THE FUTURE OF PSYCHOANALYSIS

A hundred years after the foundation of psychoanalysis it is necessary to re-evaluate its position in the modern world and think about its future. The editor of this volume is guided by the conviction that psychoanalysis as a science of man is not only an important therapeutic procedure whose innovations have provided new insights into the human mind, but also a new and even more significant contribution to a theory of culture and critique of society. The authors discuss the various new developments in therapeutic methods, and some of them refer to the discussions of the New York Psychoanalytic Institute during the 1970s. In the debates about a crisis of psychoanalysis which have been going on in the psychoanalytical community for the last twenty years, some have called for renewed solidarity with the traditional paradigmata, others demand radical reforms of the training methods and the ending of the self-ghettoization of the psychoanalytic institutes.

The authors of this book provide a thoroughgoing investigation into the nature of the crisis and propose ways to resolve it. They view the prognosis for psychoanalysis as a profession as not particularly brilliant and call for major changes in the rules of the psychoanalytic institutes in order to give their members greater freedom to form fresh ideas and discuss new adaptations of therapeutic methods to meet the changing expectations of the modern world. However, their prognosis for psychoanalysis as a human science is more favourable, but they maintain that it will need a great amount of determination and radical reforms for psychoanalysis to act 'as an important stimulant in cultural and social developments' (Freud, 1924). What these reforms should look like is one of the main themes discussed in this volume.

Contents

Foreword

In the year marking the 100th anniversary of the birth of psychoanalysis, the authors of the essays in this volume all try and discern what the future of the discipline will be.

As editor of this book I endeavoured to approach not only practising psychoanalysts, but also authors who, while outside the domain of psychoanalytical practice, have for years concerned themselves with psychoanalysis as the science of humankind, as cultural theory, and as social critique – one a philosopher, one a cultural critic, and one a sociologist. I felt this to be important, as I am of the opinion that psychoanalysis as the science of humankind must extend far beyond the borders of the current medical care system.

The five practising analysts, teachers and scholars are all active in clinical psychotherapy or psychoanalysis, and focus on the topic from the angle dictated by the respective school of thought to which they belong and in light of the differing experiences they have made. One of them tackles the issue from the vantage point of a debate which was held at the New York Psychoanalytical Institute back in the 1970s. His essay demonstrates for just how long the issue has already been a subject of discussion.

The authors do not believe that there is a rosy future for institutional psychoanalysis or the profession of analyst, let alone the standing of psychoanalysis in society. Yet they are, by contrast, of the opinion that there is a future for psychoanalysis as the science of humankind. For this science to realise its potential and for psychoanalysis to become 'a significant ferment in cultural development' (Freud, 1924) in the new century ahead, great effort and profound reforms are necessary. The shape they could take is one of the topics of the present volume.

JOHANNES CREMERIUS

i

Johannes Cremerius

The Future of Psychoanalysis

In 1924, in his *Short Account of Psychoanalysis* Freud forecast that 'psychoanalysis will become a significant ferment in the cultural development of the next few decades and will help to give our understanding of the world greater depth.' What Freud had expected was anticipated by Carl J. Burckhardt a year later: 'This man Freud will become far more powerful in the course of our century than anything which ostensibly surrounded us firmly during our childhood.' (Letter to Hugo von Hofmannsthal, Hofmannsthal-Burckhardt, 1956).

In the year in which psychoanalysis celebrates its 100th anniversary, I note with the benefit of hindsight that Freud's expectations and Burckhardt's premonition have come true for the period in question. Psychoanalysis as an idea has celebrated a triumphal forward march, exerting an unparalleled influence on the thought of scholars and on their research methods, not to mention on the works of poets, authors and artists. Psychoanalysis has, moreover, been widely, if controversially, received in the humanities. It has profoundly changed disciplines such as sociology and ethnology. It is applied practically in criminal law and has, above all, led in many places to a fundamental change in the sentences passed down on young delinquents. Literary theory endeavours to use it to find new ways of interpreting texts. Many are also the efforts to build a bridge between psychoanalysis and politics – as are the links between psychoanalysis and the Protestant and Catholic faiths (Cremerius, 1981). Nowhere has the reception been as widespread as in the works of authors and poets (Cremerius, 1987, 1993). Freud once remarked that his case studies read like novellas; and for the last ninety years, novellas and novels have read like case studies. I would refer the reader here to a prototype of such literature, Robert Musil's *Man Without Qualities* (Cremerius, 1979).

Psychoanalysis is in a phase in which incommensurable events are occurring synchronously.

3

On the brink of the new millennium, the question arises as to the future of psychoanalysis, of psychoanalysis as an idea, and of psycho-analysis as an institution. In the first section of this article, I shall focus on the future of psychoanalysis as an institution, and in the second section I shall turn to its future as an idea. In both cases, I have the good fortune to not have to depend on mere assumptions. This is true in particular as regards the future of the institution. Here, an analysis of the state of things now suffices in order to provide a reliable forecast. Since the present state has continued unchanged for decades, indeed since the foundation of the psychoanalytical movement in 1910, I can refer to something which is already history. In other words, I do not have to build my argument on the coincidental and fleeting nature of an evanescent up-to-date reality.

My prognosis for the *future of psychoanalysis as an idea*, as the science of humankind, can rely on the trends of the last twenty years. By extrapolating them I can paint a picture of their future. I shall allow myself to include in this picture my own notions of what psychoanalysis must do in order to achieve – as idea, as science – what I wish for it, namely a future status in alliance with other humanistic sciences of man.

Worries given the threatening situation facing psychoanalysis as an institution

The current state of institutional psychoanalysis is so troubling that it has been the object of countless publications on the future of psycho-analysis. In 1988, the editors of *Psychoanalytic Quarterly* invited eight of 'the profession's leaders' to comment on the future of psychoanalysis (see Nos. 57 and 58, 1988 and 1989). In 1988, Sandler held a lecture with the same title, followed a year later by Wallerstein (Sandler, 1990; Wallerstein, 1991a). In Germany, analysts who were members of the Bernfeld circle shared these worries. They joined ranks with Swiss, English, French and Italian analysts to form a group named 'Network'; in 1991-2, the Zurich Seminar of Psychoanalysis organised a lecture series on the topic of 'The Finiteness of Psychoanalysis' (1992), in the context of which I spoke on the 'Future of Psychoanalysis' (Cremerius, 1992); in 1993, Kernberg published an essay entitled *Current Problems in Psychoanalysis*, investigating the causes of the crisis and offering a 'new appraisal' of them (Kernberg, 1993).

In the main, the articles on the crisis in psychoanalysis published from the middle of this century onwards (e.g. Fromm, 1970; Kohut, 1973) did not attract much attention. Even the voice of so renowned an author as Eissler, who prophesied 'no glorious future' for psychoanalysis (Eissler, 1965, p.469) went unheeded, as did the efforts by the *Revue française de Psychanalyse* in 1975 to address the topic with due gravity. The book in which Eissler presented his worries went unremarked and has still not been translated into German; the essays in the *Revue* were not the subject of discussion in Germany at all. The efforts by the Bernfeld circle and the 'Network' ten years later, although initially attracting attention, have in the final instance not set anything in motion in the ossified institution itself.

In contrast to this refusal to square up to these efforts to identify a crisis, the essays in *Psychoanalytic Quarterly* were taken into account. However, they also did not provide the basis for a strong solution. On the one hand, this was due to the fact that institutional psychoanalysis – and the articles all focused on the threat to precisely this – did not find it necessary to make the issue the topic for meetings or conferences, and, on the other, because the authors in the *Quarterly* tried to identify the causes of the 'dangerous changes in our science and our profession' outside institutional psychoanalysis, in other words in an area which psychoanalysis as an institution was unable to influence. They found the cause in:

- the increase in alternative therapy forms and the related worry that psychoanalysts would lose patients to the former;
- the decrease in enrolments at the training institutes, above all the marked fall in doctors who wished to become professional psychoanalysts;
- the switch from a dynamic outlook in psychiatry to an approach rooted predominantly in biology and behavioural therapy;
- the growing willingness of the population to trust in pharmacological forms of therapy under the guidance of their family doctor. The result is that many patients requiring therapy never even reach the consulting room;
- the discontinuation of state support;
- the loss of prestige enjoyed by psychoanalysis in US society;
- the disappointment with psychoanalysis as regards both its curative effect and its ability to change society;
- the resistance to its elitist stance, 'malevolent criticism' and animosity.

This outward-directed view away from the profession prevented the diagnosticians from discerning the internal causes of the crisis and this, in turn, rendered them incapable of considering how such phenomena could be best dealt with. I shall endeavour to focus on the internal causes. What first strikes the eye given such a change in emphasis is that cause and effect are inverted. What the above-mentioned diagnosticians consider exclusively to be causes of the problem are essentially the effects of problems and failings within the profession; are above all the consequence of the self-alienation of psychoanalysis as a consequence of its having abandoned the principles which forged its identity.

The failure to come to terms with the pre-history of institutional psychoanalysis

All ideas start as heresy and end as dogma.

In order to be able to understand these problems and failings, as well as the self-alienated state of psychoanalysis, we must know its prehistory, its origins in the spirit of the 'psychoanalytic movement', a spirit which goes sharply against the grain of the principles of psychoanalysis, namely liberation through enlightenment. We can find unpleasant traces leading from those early days in our present times. Those days back in March 1910 when the psychoanalytical movement was founded in Nuremberg, transpire not to have been glory days. Instead, they saw the foundations laid for the authoritarian and hierarchical structure of the International Psychoanalytical Association (IPA): The President was to be the father whose claims were incontrovertible and whose authority was inviolable. The movement required a 'head' with far-reaching power (Jones 1995, vol. II, p.90) and an organ which controlled the members. Moreover, the President was to be furnished with extraordinary authority, including that to appoint or dismiss analysts and authorise all publications by members on psychoanalysis prior to their appearing (*ibid.*). By accepting this formulation and by his later behaviour Freud merely fostered this structure. For example, he set out the goals and purposes of psychoanalytical training in a quite ideologically coercive manner (see below, p.9). In order to protect his ideas against the passage of time he founded a 'committee', a 'sort of old guard', intended to 'defend the cause against personalities and accidents, when I am no more.' (Jones, 1955, p.173f.) He then founded 'local groups' in the capitals of the world, whose directors had to have submitted to analysis by him in person, with the object of ensuring that his oeuvre survived the passage of time; he called them 'colonists'. The definition of certain strands of the theory as maxims was also intended to counteract transience. Tellingly, he spoke of shibboleths (passwords that allow one to differentiate friend from foe) and of a 'holy rule'. Anyone not prepared to approve of the shibboleths should, he wrote in 1923, not consider themselves psychoanalysts (Freud, 1923a, p.223). Given an environment which Freud and his pupils felt was inimical to them, they closed ranks in a sort of self-ghettoization[1] and isolated themselves from the world, gathering around a founding father who said of himself in 1914: 'Psychoanalysis is my creation.'[2] Like Karl Marx, that other great 19th century innovator, Freud, as the founder of psychoanalysis, feared that his idea would only survive if he protected it, like Marx before him, by means of an 'International', an authoritarian and hierarchically structured organisation. In both cases, the opposite actually happened. Although the 'Psychoanalytical International' gained international power, Freud's ideas were largely sacrificed at the altar of this power and its perpetuation. It no longer exercises the functions which once so imbued it with meaning, namely the wish to keep an enlightened, socio-critical science alive. It has become an anachronism (Erdheim, 1987). What has survived of it is 'psychoanalysis in chains'.

The organisational structure that I have outlined accords with that which Popper described by means of the term 'closed society' (Popper, 1942).

Psychoanalytical Training – Somewhere between Vocational College and Theological Seminary

> The psychoanalytical community has still not worked through this inheritance, has not yet squared up to its own history. It is now forced to repeat it.
>
> Two elements from the history of psychoanalysis still had an effect today, said Knight in his address as President of the APA: the clinging attitude of disciples in the context of idolisation and the idea of the psycho-analytical movement as an instrument of political power (Knight, 1953, p.211; his predecessor had made similar remarks as president of the APA: Cooper, 1984).

7

The very day psychoanalysis as an institution decided to give its system of education a bureaucratic organisation – in the form of the Berlin Psychoanalytical Institute (BPI) in 1925 – it simultaneously placed it in the service of this 'closed system', the 'church', as Graf and Sachs term it. Admission procedures, the training analysis and the curriculum became its cornerstones. The *admission procedures* are similar to those which ordination candidates face when wishing to enter a seminary (see Kernberg, 1984) in that applicants have to endure informal interviews and are therefore subject to the tyranny of the person conducting the interview. In the case of abuse, there is no supra-ordinated agency with which complaints can be lodged. The ideological basis of this initiation is evidenced by the fact that all attempts to change it have been doomed to failure. Even Anna Freud's authority proved powerless in this regard. The procedure, she asserted, could not be combined 'with respect for the individual personality' (A. Freud, 1966, p.227f.) The fact that in the 70 years the procedure has been used, its efficacy has never been subjected to stringent examination, let alone proved to this day,[3] is merely a further indication of this ideological background. Balint has noted that in the period up until the end of the Second World War there were no publications which dealt with the personal qualifications of applicants for admission to training (Balint, 1947). As a consequence, selection was by means of what Bernfeld calls a 'primitive-physio-gnomic method' (Bernfeld, 1962, p.450), i.e. according to the method: he is like me – or not like me. Balint's observation should not be read to mean that there was no focus on selection issues. There most certainly was, but 'behind closed doors'.

So what is the link between the shortcomings of the procedure and the crisis of the institution? They are linked by the fact that the selection procedure is a pseudo selection procedure and accordingly does not guarantee the quality of those admitted to the profession. Anna Freud remarked: 'The type preferred by today's [1972] teaching institutes is a conformist; he is rather more diligent in reality and harder-working than he is by inclination perspicacious and creative.' (Anna Freud, 1972, p.21) Hanns Sachs believed the consequences this had for the profession were far graver: 'It is paradoxical that there is a group which is unfit for the career of an analyst because there are too few psychoneurotic symptoms. ... Its freedom from discernible neurotic symptoms depends on firm repression with consequent inability to reach the unconscious and incapacity for understanding its utterances ... It is hardly necessary to add that this remoteness from their own unconscious excludes any real understanding of the unconscious of others.' (Sachs, 1947, p.161) Sachs goes on to ask why such persons should be trained to pursue a profession for which they were currently not particularly well equipped to pursue and probably never were going to be. In the mid-1920s, Freud furthered tersely: 'The good are worthless and the disobedient leave.' (Roazen, 1976, p.301)

Despite these warnings, the procedure is still upheld. It explains the great number of 'normopaths' (Bird, 1968), of 'imitation candidates' (Gaddini, 1984) and of 'dull normal people' (Kernberg, 1984, p.23) who pass through the admissions procedure – to the detriment of the profession and of psychoanalytical scholarship. There is a clear reference here to the low scholarly and scientific level of the psychoanalytical association (see below, pp.10 & 11).

Training analysis serves the interests of the 'Church' even more so than does the admissions procedure. Freud himself it was who determined that training fulfil this purpose. Training analysis[4], he opined, should serve to more or less counteract the 'personal equation' of the analysand, so that one day fairly satisfactory agreements could be reached among analysts (Freud, 1926e, SE vol XX, p.220). The originally purposeful idea of developing a teaching-and-learning method tailored to the specific needs of the profession of analyst was undermined by this intention (Cremerius, 1989). In the final instance, it degenerated into a state where 'independent candidates became enthusiastic proselytes' (Balint, 1947, p.326) and 'credulous analysts' (Wildlöcher, 1983). In other words, training analysis got what in Sachs' opinion it needed, namely something 'that corresponded to the status of novices in the Church' (Sachs, 1930).

The critical voices to be heard today indicate that the old intention of abusing training analysis for the purposes of indoctrination and alienating it from its real purpose still persists. In 1947, Balint described training analysis as an initiation rite which, like all initiation rites, had the goal of forcing the newcomer to identify with the clan (Balint, 1947). Other commentators have agreed with this criticism. In 1950, Anna Freud repeated the criticism she had voiced in 1938, stating that training analysis was 'non-rite analysis' (A. Freud, 1938/1950) or, in an even more trenchant note in 1976 'wild analysis' (A. Freud, 1976, p.2805) which therefore culminated in poor results and unresolved attachment based on transference (1938, 1950). In 1962, Bernfeld termed training analysis 'non-Freudian analysis' (Bernfeld, 1962). In 1967, McLaughlin weighed in by asking 'what motivates us to use persistently a model which we otherwise hold to be unanalytic?' and Limentani, at the time President of the IPA, stated: 'I believe that taking someone into a so-called training analysis, we perpetuate a devastating attack on the setting, quite apart from creating transference and counter-transference problems' (Limentani, 1986). Eissler believed 'the symbolic killing of the son' was the motif to be discerned in the element of subjection inherent in such training analysis. Despite this criticism, training analysis in the old form has been given an ever stronger basis. Indeed, the fact that it has continually been extended in duration (today it entails 1,000 or more hours, in four or five sessions a week, whereas in 1933 it only lasted one or one and a half years) entails the danger that the above-mentioned damage (indoctrination, a lack of success and undissolved libidinal attachment based on tranference) continues to increase[5].

What exactly is the connection between these shortcomings of training analysis and the crisis of psychoanalysis as an institution? On the one hand, the infantile attachment, the unresolved oedipus complex with its ambivalent feelings, permits no thought without prejudice, no freedom of choice (if the oedipus complex is not worked through, the cognitive level drops). This inhibition of thought constrains the development of a scholarly community, which is after all what psychoanalysis as an institution wishes to be. (Seen differently, 'the church' benefits from this, for constrained thought benefits belief.) Anna Freud pointed to this problem back in 1938 and identified unresolved transference (onto the teaching analyst) as the cause of an insufficiently scientific attitude on the part of the candidates (A. Freud, 1938/1950). This limitation of scientific and scholarly thought is reflected in the low scholarly level of the IPA. After 40 years of efforts by renowned analysts, or so Wallerstein avers, there had still been no movement as regards scholarly advances (Wallerstein, 1991). The commission set up by the IPA with the brief to establish why 'there is a lack of new psychoanalytic insights in the central areas of analytical knowledge' (Kohut, 1969) bore no fruit. Their findings brought no increase in scientific impulses, in freedom in the psychoanalytical doctrine; nor did it lead to the institutes opening their doors to related sciences. Instead, it culminated in greater narrow-mindedness, above all as regards the selection criteria for the training curriculum (Kohut, *ibid.*; cf. also Kohut 1973/75). It is an old complaint; after all, Franz Alexander already identified this shortcoming in 1957 (Alexander, 1957). What is worth noting is that Wallerstein, and also others such as Edelson (1988) and Kernberg (1993) who speak of a scientific deficit, do not expressly establish a link between low academic standards and training analysis. Klauber seems to be an exception here. He writes: 'Identity formation by the analyst adheres to the pattern of religious conversion.' (Klauber, 1980) Just how true this is can be seen from the way Kohut's ideas spread in West Germany in the early 1970s. They prompted something like an 'inspirational movement' which swept through entire analytic centres 'like an epidemic' (Jappe, 1983). Another link between training analysis, 'wild psychoanalysis' and the crisis of the institution is to be seen in the permanent schisms in the international psychoanalytic community and the numerous movements which have turned their backs on it[6].

These originate in training analysis, when a substantial part of the analysis – namely the working out of aggression, anger and jealousy – is not possible, because the teaching analyst doubles up as representative of the institution into which the analysand wishes to gain entry[7]. Be it a real fact or merely imagined, entry into the institution depends on the teaching analyst[8]. The fear of annoying the analyst by negative transference is consequently understandable as such. In many countries it is a real fear. In five IPA member associations (Barcelona, England, Denmark, Norway, Vienna), the teaching analyst still intervenes in the decisions of the teaching committee, as was the case after 1925 at the Berlin Psychoanalytical Institute. The analyst contributes a judgement of the progress made by the analysand and the candidate's suitability. These reports are made either every six months or on an *ad hoc* basis. As late as 1994, the European Conference on Questions of Training debated whether teaching analysts should be permitted to submit reports or not.

As a rule, unresolved transference onto the teaching analyst typically ends in two ways: on the one hand, rebellion, protest, separation; and, on the other, identification. The latter is the cause of what Balint has termed 'clan building' around the teaching analyst.

Finally, the disproportionate role self-experience plays in the institutes – in other words the preponderance of teaching analysis (four hours a week plus travel time, over a total of five to seven years) – necessarily helps cause the institutes increasingly to become ghettoes, as the process separates the candidates from the outside world and promotes their retreat into the internal world of the institute. (In other words, I thus establish a causal link between the self-ghettoization of psychoanalysis and teaching analysis.) It is far harder for both to occur in an open institute with lively interdisciplinary activities. This retreat into introspection explains, or so I suspect, why world-wide we are witnessing a decreasing interest in Freud's writings on cultural theory and his critique of society; indeed, in some quarters there is no interest in them at all. This lack of interest has led to analysts today being reluctant to comment on social issues or topics of the day (with a few notable exceptions such as Parin and Richter; see Parin, 1978). Topics of the day are considered to be incompatible with the role of the analyst as he would only declaim his personal political or religious opinion or view of the world and would thus shed the anonymity required of him to the detriment of his patients (transference problems).

This is certainly not the only reason for the silence. Rather, this stance among individuals reflects the inclination in the psychoanalytical community not to interfere, and instead to conform. In the United States, the community has conformed to the official school of thinking in medicine, in Germany after 1933 it adjusted to conform with German psychiatry, and in West Germany to conform with the constraints of the German health service. The IPA kept its silence on the Vietnam War and on other wars, on the oppression of minorities (blacks and gays), on the prohibition of *coitus interruptus*, on the misery facing children (violence towards children and sexual abuse of children) and on the misery of unemployed adolescents. As early as 1962, Adorno remarked critically that analysts in the United States (and this is true of Europe today) has long since sworn an oath of fealty to the predominant prototypical culture there and had by means of self-castration smoothed the way for rendering psychoanalysis conventional.

Freud did not share this concern of today's analysts. He publicly and unequivocally took a stance against war (he signed the appeal against war organised by Henry Barbuse and Romain Rolland in 1927), in favour of peace, in favour of pacifism (in 1917 and 1930), of religion (1930), of socialism and communism (1930). He was a Board Member of the Austrian section of the 'League for the Protection of Mothers' founded in 1905 by Helene Stoecker, which was soon to call itself 'League for the Protection of Mothers and Sexual Reform'. The league's goals were to combat the moral and legal condemnation of unmarried mothers and illegitimate children, male double standards, and anti-abortion laws. In 1908, Freud published two articles in the league's 'Mutterschutz' journal: *'Civilised' Sexual Morality and Modern Nervous Illness* and *On the Sexual Theories of Children*. In 1927, the Vienna *Arbeiterzeitung* brought out a manifesto calling for support for the social policy pursued by the Social Democrats, above all the efforts to reform tax laws. The list of signatories of the appeal was led not only by Alfred

Adler and Karl Blücher, but also by Sigmund Freud. However, we need to qualify these remarks: Freud always departed from this approach if he believed it would jeopardise his life's work. When the danger became acute in 1933, he hoped his absolute neutrality would save the Berlin Psychoanalytic Institute. So worried was he that he spoke out against members of DPG, the German Psychoanalytic Society, being politically active, whether in left-wing groups or in explicitly anti-fascist groups. Thereafter, DPG members who were members of the 'League of Socialist Doctors' and the German Communist Party had to meet in secret and live out the political part of their lives underground (see Jacoby, 1983, and Langer, 1986).

We can find traces of the 'Church' in the *basis of training* itself, namely in the *curriculum*. The relationship to the founding fathers has not been resolved (and here we find repeated the pattern which we have seen obtaining between training analyst and training analysand). This means that it is not possible 'to view psychoanalysis as a science of the mind' (Knight, 1953, p.211) and compels us to 'guard it as dogma'. As long as this is the case, A.N. Whitehead's maxim applies that 'a science which hesitates to forget its founder is lost' (quoted in Merton, 1962, p.3). And this is truly the case. In training, Freud's writings are still studied chronologically instead of critically from today's point of view (Wallerstein, 1989, p.356). They are not juxtaposed to more recent texts, such as those by Schäfer, George S. Klein, Peterfreund, Gill, Weiss, and Sampson – all of them honourable members of the IPA. When I myself was undergoing training, Freud's clinical studies were read as doctrine and not, as should have been the case, 'against the grain'. At numerous training institutes today, many semesters are still spent 'practising the acrobatics of energy transformation, as if these things bore a direct relation to clinical work' (Sandler, 1983, p.582). A further problem is that Freud's writings are almost exclusively studied in preparation for practical work. Students no longer tussle with their theoretical substance, i.e. their philosophical thrust. Yet Freud himself believed precisely such a study was important. For psychoanalysis was meant to be more than merely the therapeutic treatment of neurosis, more than an 'auxiliary science in the field of psychopathology'. It was meant to be 'the starting point of a new and deeper science of the mind'; 'a path lay open to it that led far afield, into spheres of universal interest.' (Freud, 1925, SE vol. X, p.47). In 1933 he said, '...I did not want to commend it [psychoanalysis] to your interest as a method of treatment but on account of the truths it contains, on account of the information it gives us about what concerns human beings most of all – their own nature...' (*New Lectures*, SE vol. XXII, pp 156-7). But not only the 'exhaustive psychology' is being neglected. The same is true of Freud's socio-critical writings, as the curricula at the most DPV institutes readily reveal. This reflects the psychoanalytical community's wish to forgo the socio-political potential of psychoanalysis and its fear about concerning itself with its own history in society. Only at a very late date did psychoanalysis investigate its role during the Third Reich (Lohmann & Rosenkötter, 1982). Until light was shed on its problematic past under the Nazis, the issue of the Third Reich was hardly ever mentioned in the DPV. When I underwent my second analysis in Zurich from 1960 to 1963 – and several German analysts were there doing the same at that time – the Swiss analysts noticed that the topic of fascism had hardly been elaborated on in the first course of analysis (all the analysands I knew were of a generation which had experienced fascism personally). And even today this issue is largely ignored – something I note when myself conducting second analyses.

Kernberg complains that the science of psychoanalysis has been eroded by the limitations on scholarly work imposed by the organisation of psychoanalytical institutes (Kernberg, 1993).

The psychoanalytical institution bears the traits of a 'Church'

> Where religions become churches and political ideas parties, preserving the institution becomes more important than upholding the functions which originally gave them meaning.
>
> 'In the space of a few years I experienced the entire history of the Church.'
> Max Graf looking back on his years with Freud (1942)

As I have frequently observed an analogy between the IPA's organisational form and training system, on the one hand, and a religious community or 'Church', on the other, I should like to go into this more closely. As mentioned above (p.7), there is a similarity between Freud and the founding figures of 'Churches'. He created the doctrine ('Psychoanalysis is my creation'); he was a charismatic leader; he held psychoanalysis to be the truth ('We possess the truth'); he ordained that parts of the doctrine were shibboleths and 'holy rules' ('anyone not wishing to accept them all should not consider himself a psychoanalyst').

And he felt that, like a missionary, he had to convert others: the analysts he had personally analysed were to represent psychoanalysis as its 'regional group heads' in the world's metropolises. What he wanted to see was a 'psychoanalytic movement', a psychoanalytic international that would guarantee that the public was offered 'real psychoanalysis', that the latter was protected 'against imitations', and which served as a central agency in the struggle with the foe (letter to Eugen Bleuer, 1910, quoted in: Clark, 1979, p.331f.). To safeguard this 'movement' he founded a committee meant to defend his life's work after his death. The existence and the influence of the committee was meant to remain completely secret. He organised a training system which revolved around a method, namely training analysis, which had the goal of 'creating a satisfactory degree of concurrence among the analysts.' This can be read to mean the production of proselytes. Hanns Sachs has described the situation among members of the psychoanalytical movements as follows. He first notes that they are subject to the strictest rules, regulations and limitations, and goes on to say: 'Everything from the small details of everyday routine to the most momentous decisions was shaped by [Freud's] dictation.' (Sachs, 1945, p.70) Eitingon reports that the goal of the association is to 'preserve what our master created – against premature additions and so-called syntheses with other areas and differently structured research and working methods' (Eitingon, 1925, p.516)

If knowledge becomes a dogmatic certainty, then all deviance has to be suppressed and persecuted. Freud and his disciples made certain that deviants were immediately identified as such and condemned for their apostasy. Freud wrote to Sabina Spielrein after she had become a member of the Viennese Psychoanalytical Association: 'If you stay with us, you will have to see the enemy over there [with Jung];' (Cremerius, 1986). Max Graf, the father of 'little Hans', wrote that 'Freud insisted … that if one followed Adler … one was no more a Freudian' (Graf, 1942, p.473) The list of those condemned for apostasy is long. Even old and loyal pupils such as Ferenczi suffered this fate. In 1927, it was Melanie Klein's turn to be on the receiving end. Freud wrote at the time: '[Your ideas] are in complete contradiction to all my basic assumptions … I strongly contest the validity of your interpretations' [quote slightly modified]. (Steiner, 1985, pp. 31 & 37). And this verdict was to lead to her expulsion from the IPA – or so the proposal submitted by Anna Freud and her friends in 1945, which was then rejected.

The IPA has also remained a high church after the founding years.

The association is still authoritarian and hierarchical in structure (see below, p.17 on the 'Altenburger Paper'). Training analysis continues to be part of the curriculum and in several countries it is subject to close monitoring, with the analyst reporting in secret. In other words, the principle of secrecy persists. Resolutions on the candidates are still made behind closed doors; it was not until 1983 that all training analysts were allowed to participate in the preliminary congresses on training issues. The circle of those invited to attend was, however, restricted to a few delegates. Only the committee handling the invitations knew the criteria for the selection. Moreover, the reputed psychoanalytic publishing organs refer to an editorial committee whose members remain unknown to those submitting manuscripts. The committee controls what may be printed and what may not, without informing the authors of the reasons for the respective decision[9]. As in a secret sect, when analytical congresses take place, the general public is strictly excluded from attending, only members and candidates undergoing training are allowed to participate – as are a few guests recommended by well-known analysts. With an almost religious rejection of everything foreign and a semi-phobic refusal to heed the findings of other scientific disciplines, psychoanalysis still exists in a ghetto it has itself erected.

This stance leads to the academic establishment rejecting psychoanalysis. Jaspers was one of them (Jaspers, 1951). Today, scientists with whom the IPA wishes to enter into dialogue respond with the same answers as those Eugen Bleuer trooped out in 1910 when Freud approached him: 'For me [your] theory is only one new truth among other truths.' Freud's principle of 'all or nothing' was 'necessary for religious sects and for political parties … but [harmful] for science.' (Alexander & Seleneski, 1965, p.5).

Religious structures are impervious to criticism, whether from the outside or from the inside. Even the founder of the entire structure, namely Freud himself, had to discover this, when in 1927 he protested against the exclusion of laypersons from the psychoanalytical community. Brill threatened to terminate their friendship, and Freud had to give in – in the interests of the very community which was in the process of destroying it anyway (Cremerius, 1986). Where no criticism is possible there is also no complaints board. All decisions on admission to training, performance and conclusion of the courses, or so the candidates' assembly of the IPA complained, were vague and imprecise and there were no legal means to rectify wrongdoings (Franzen, 1982; see also Speier, 1983). Kernberg describes the 'paranoid atmosphere' which he feels rules in the IPA's training institutions, alongside a continual 'threat of persecution' (Kernberg, 1984, p.561). One of the first known examples of the defencelessness of candidates undergoing training is the afore-mentioned case of Margaret Mahler. When her teaching analyst, Helene Deutsch, prematurely discontinued the analysis because Mahler was ostensibly 'unanalysable', she was unable to defend herself against this judgement and had to break off her training (Stepansky, 1989, p.88).

And there is yet another parallel between the IPA and a church. In both, women do not manage to penetrate the uppermost echelons. Since its foundation in 1910, only once has a woman been, briefly, president of the IPA – and then only as a substitute for a man who was unable to discharge his duties. The dominance of the men is impressively reflected in the relation of male to female training analysts in the DPV: 75 per cent are men, 25 per cent are women.

Finally, like a high Church, the IPA resorts to coercive measures. It has to if it wishes to maintain the community of believers and the training system which buttresses this community. Such steps include threatening teaching analysts with expulsion. Teaching analysts who show signs of deviating significantly from the psychoanalytic theory and practice have to report this themselves or others are expected to report it in order for them to be released from their activities (Altenburg Paper, 1985). Then there is the ' incompatibility clause'. 'The participation in special courses of further training in order to acquire the additional qualification for practising psychoanalysis is not compatible with the associated purpose of the German PA' (Resolution of the General Assembly of the DPV, 1986). And these sentences are not just ink on paper. Fonagy states that Sandler felt it was important during his period of office as president of the IPA to point again and again to the dangers threatening the identity of psychoanalysis posed by IPA analysts taking part in forms of training for psychotherapy and in the professional psychotherapy associations (Fonagy, 1993). Is it not a matter of denial if DPV analysts earn their living through psychotherapy and yet, for reasons of identity, are not permitted to teach psychotherapy? The IPA has also upheld the first coercive measure it applied, used back in 1925, and still practises it today, namely compulsory membership (Wittenberger, 1987). Accordingly, you do not become an analyst by dint of completing psychoanalytical training at an IPA institute, but only by membership of the IPA, something one automatically receives on successfully passing the oral examination. In other words, there is no choice. If someone rejects membership, they have to expressly declare that they do not wish to become a member. Loch asserts that an analyst receives his or her identity as an analyst only by dint of sanctioning from the outside in the form of entry into the psychoanalytical community, that is into the IPA (Loch 1974; see also Sandler, 1989, in particular p. 38).

As a scholarly discipline, psychoanalysis has no future if bound to this organizational form. For a science, theories are only suggestions for ways of seeing things. As a religious community it cannot take such a view but instead requires metaphors, symbols and meta-theoretical speculations 'beyond the domain of empirical research', speculation with which we live as 'the articles of our faith' (Wallerstein, 1988).

Institutionalised psychoanalysis turns its back on the fundamental psychoanalytical premisses

> Institutionalised psychoanalysis destroys what it wished to preserve. 'I have seen the enemy, and we are he.'
> (Golding)

In a quite unprecedented process of purgation the psychoanalytical institution has divested itself of its real function and left Freud's demand that it be an emancipatory enlightening science well behind it. In his *Future Prospects of Psycho-Analytical Therapy* (1910d) Freud wrote programmatically that psychoanalysis can only lay claim to authority in the world if 'we take a critical stance towards society,' and in 1921 he added in *Psychoanalysis and Telepathy* (Freud 1941d) that psychoanalysis must oppose 'all the conventionally restricted, predetermined and generally accepted' and must disturb the peace of this world (Freud 1916/1917, SE vol. XVI p.285).

Instead, in the course of what Parin has termed a 'process of purgation' (1986) institutionalised psychoanalysis has shed precisely what once constituted its oppositional core:

- the irritation of the sexual, instinct theory;
- the 'emancipatory mission of psychoanalysis' (Parin, 1978, p.655). The curriculum of DPV institutes hardly any longer touch on Freud's cultural theory and social critique. The concepts of culture and cultural critique no longer crop up in psychoanalytical vocabulary and monographs;
- the social factors which (help) cause and promote neurosis. In their

place, factors are now addressed such as congenital properties (Melanie Klein) or the coincidences of constellations in the first few
months of early childhood: mother as fate (Kohut). Now, society is
freed of the burden it carried. For if the fate of a person is determined during the first two years of its life, then sexual development
through until adolescence is of lesser significance;

- Freud's theory of object relations. His 'frightening' assertion that
an instinctual drive does not seek out a special object of love, a
'thou', but rather a random 'sexual goal' if this only serves to discharge sexual tension;

- lay analysis, which Freud regarded as an indispensable part of his
conception of the psychoanalytical community. And for good reason.
He wished the psychoanalytical community to remain embedded in
the mainstream of European intellectual history and for philosophy,
the psychology of religion, ethnology, literary studies, etc. to be
taught at its training institutes – he speaks of 'psychoanalytical
colleges'. 'Unless he is well at home in these subjects, an analyst
can make nothing of a large amount of his material' (*Two Short
Accounts*, p.165). If 'laypersons' are admitted to training, their knowledge of these subjects serves to enrich the training sessions. (In
their lectures, doctors only rarely impart cultural theory.) Freud
believed that the presence of laypersons would ensure a counter-
balance to a centering on the medical side. Perhaps he also hoped
that the consequent interdisciplinary approach would form a counterweight to the isolation of the institutes. (Here we see Freud caught
up in his own contradictions.)[10]

The Self-Destruction of Psychoanalysis by its Fixation on an Anachronistic Position

The deliberate restriction of therapy to members of the educated
and affluent middle classes is self-destructive, as is the exclusion of
exogenous influences on the development of neuroses, an aspect which
Freud believed to be of great importance. Thanks to this restriction
psychoanalysis seals itself off from social reality and becomes ana-
chronistic. As a consequence, it is able neither to perceive social changes
nor to relate these as problems to its own theoretical framework or
treatment practices. The exclusion of exogenous factors serves to bind
psychoanalysis to a mono-causal patho-etiological model which does
not do justice to the reality of the reasons for human suffering. In this

19

context, institutionalised psychoanalysis is unable to perceive the changes in interpersonal relationships and the changed position of people in a pluralistic world of different lifestyles. Instead it still sees the world through 19th century eyes.

Class-specific analysis prevents analysts having experience of patients from a different social stratum and with a different level of education, patients who are not able to pay for their therapy themselves or whose therapy is paid for by a third party (a health insurance company or national health scheme)[11]. Eissler comments on this as follows: 'I anticipate such a benefit in two areas: it will broaden the analyst's knowledge of social groups which exist in his community, and would protect him against a one-sided view of the social structure and its impact on the individual. Furthermore, it would enable him to accumulate experiences from analyses in which the fee factor plays no role as a motivating force (either in the patient or in the analyst) and should thus not only contribute to the refinement of the psychoanalytic technique but also solidify and maintain the psychoanalyst's own freedom and independence from the impact which the monetary factor may gradually exert on him ...' (Eissler, 1974, p.85). I would like to add that restricting psychoanalysis to patients capable of paying for the treatment themselves is also to the detriment of institutionalised psychoanalysis, which thus bars itself from taking part in the broad psychotherapeutic and psychoanalytical care for the population as a whole. Back in 1919 Freud expressed the wish that in the future psychoanalysis play such a part, providing 'psychotherapy for the people' with psychoanalytical underpinnings (Freud, 1919). I believe that the restriction to private patients and to highly frequent sessions during a long-term course of psychoanalysis does not guarantee a promising future to the institution of psychoanalysis which raises such a form of therapy to the level of a principle.

The *exclusion of exogenous factors*, in other words the dismissal of social factors (social misery and privation, unemployment, the hopelessness of young people without a future, the loss of personality in the media society, etc.) and the impact these conditions have on psychological health renders psychoanalysis a reductive, mono-etiological concept. This reduction is a product of institutionalised psychoanalysis' rigid over-emphasis on the psychological factor – the private unconscious. In 1963, at the IPA's Stockholm Congress, the IPA president demanded that analysts resist the temptation to enter social terrain. He was not able to cite Freud in his support. Freud considered the social factor an essential element in the patho-etiology of neuroses. This mono-etiological concept makes it harder to understand patients who have been damaged by society, primarily patients from a lower social stratum. And it compels these patients to seek other forms of psychotherapeutic assistance. This merely serves to emphasise the elitist position of psychoanalysis, and marginalises it in a world in which psychotherapy is increasingly part of ever more comprehensive healthcare services. It is only since analysts obsessed with intensive long-term courses of analysis have no longer found enough patients for this form of therapy that they have been compelled to assuage the situation by relying on the healthcare services. This has led directly to the discontinuation of their previous form of treatment and to an inflation in therapeutic goals[12]. The alternative, and this is gradually dawning on institutionalised psychoanalysis, is either to remain entrenched in an elitist position or to agree to its incorporation into general analytical psychotherapy as part of healthcare programmes. Neither possibility offers promising prospects.

Institutionalised psychoanalysis in a particularly drastic way rejects *the results of psychoanalytical-psychotherapeutic research* (Freud's fear of transience immediately comes to mind; Cremerius 1990b). The relationship to Freud is still one of unresolved transference and prevents institutionalised psychoanalysis from letting go of its fixation on the so-called classic technique and its rules. 'The fundamentals,' wrote Greenson in what is the standard training manual on psychoanalytical techniques, 'that Freud laid down in five short papers still serve as the basis of psychoanalytic practice (Freud 1912a, 1912b, 1913b, 1914b, 1915a). No acknowledged major changes or advances have taken hold in standard psychoanalytic technique.' (Greenson, *Technique and Practice of Psychoanalysis*, Hogarth Press, 1967 p.3). Indeed, Anna Freud was of the same opinion when she averred a decade later that the Ego psychology practised in the 1920s had not brought any major changes in the technique.

Bound up in the conviction that they possess an eternally valid method of treatment (Freud: 'We possess the truth'), the institutionalists do not consider it necessary to assess whether the method is efficient. As a consequence, efforts by renowned scholars to initiate studies on its efficacy, i.e. research into comparative psychotherapy, have been met with scepticism and widespread rejection.

By upholding this stance, institutionalised psychoanalysis has manoeuvred itself into a corner. Its demand that national health services or health insurances cover the costs of the psychoanalytical treatment are rejected because such bodies insist that the efficacy of this form of treatment be first tested or proven. References to cases where analysis has helped are all very well, but they are not recognised as proof of efficacy. Financial backers wish for objective criteria, reduction of the subjective factor, and clarification of the question whether the result could not have been achieved with a shorter, more economic procedure.

Thirdly, the absence of efforts to face up to the *changed position of people in a pluralistic world of lifestyles* and tackle it in theoretical terms is self-destructive. (Here, we again see the above-mentioned refusal to take up insights into human life gained in other disciplines, i.e. the rejection of interdisciplinary debate.) Society as Freud understood it was hierarchical and authoritarian in structure. There were levels of the hierarchy which people took as points of orientation (the emperor, the Church, bourgeois values). Today, we are witnessing a multiplication of socially accepted ways of life and the connected social values and norms. This multiplication goes hand in hand with a decay in binding, generally valid models and the concomitant moral and/or religious values and norms. This decay corresponds to the disappearance of agencies of leadership and guidance (Fürstenau, 1994, pp.40ff.). I cite here a few examples of social changes which institutionalised psychoanalysis has not worked through:

- the changed position of the father in society. A society structured hierarchically and in authoritarian terms has given way to a 'fatherless society';
- a society in which each individual him or herself bore the responsibility for curbing the risks of life (illness, age, etc.) by making the requisite provisions has, in countries with a comprehensive welfare system, been replaced by a general caring attitude – what Mitscherlich called 'collective motherhood', something which provokes an attitude of infantile and passive expectations;[13]
- the position of women in society has changed profoundly. They are searching for new forms of self-realisation and object to being 'phallically' pathologised when they actively demand and fight for the position in society to which they are entitled;
- women no longer allow themselves to be classified as 'lacking something' in terms of 'penis envy'. They turn the Freudian cause-effect model on its head: they consider what Freud termed their nature as the result of social repression;
- the relationship between children and parents has also undergone profound change, as has the position of the child in society. The

authority of parents has been weakened and they have not yet found a way of developing new forms of relationships;

- partnerships for living together (marriage), originally praised as an Ego achievement and as a sign of ability to create object constancy are no longer a value prioritised by society. In its place, bonds based on necessity such as partnerships for certain periods of life are being tried out. Object constancy is no longer a feature of a mature Ego organisation and is instead interpreted as attesting to an Ego weakness, an inability to endure separation;
- whereas in Freud's day sexuality was a private affair, shamefully concealed from view, today it is a public matter;
- in the place of the primacy of genital sexuality, which was ostensibly supra-ordinated to pre-genital sexual organisation, we now see the primacy of pre-genital sexuality (film primarily thrives on the thrill of the latter);
- while psychoanalysis still lives by the maxim that 'Where Id was, there shall Ego be', society now calls for its inversion, namely 'where Ego is, there shall Id be'.

If psychoanalysis wishes to continue to make good its claim to be a science of the human being, then it must reflect on the social reality in which people live today, relate this to its theory, and, where necessary, revise the latter. The future of analytical therapy will depend on whether it succeeds in achieving this. Should it fail, then it will, as an anachronism, come to an end.

Denying the Crisis

> Orthodoxy must change its principles instead of ignoring reality.

In the hour of deep concern, in view of the 'dangerous changes' facing 'our science and our profession', institutionalised psychoanalysis is not prepared to budge as regards reforming its head or its body. Rather, it delegates the problems to be tackled to commissions – commissions on questions of psychoanalytical technique, on the difference between psychoanalysis and psychotherapy, on clarifying the question why no more recent scientific insights have been made (see above pp.10ff.) and on the inadequacies of training analysis (see above pages 9 & 15) etc. These commissions work for decades and then at some point simply disappear without having achieved anything[14]. Then new problems arise and new commissions have to be set up, and so on. These activities resemble Tinguely's machines, which revolve so energetically without moving, and also bring to mind Lampedusa's sentence that 'What we want is for everything to remain the way it is, for it is necessary for everything to change.'

> 'We welcome illusions because they spare us unplea-
> surable feelings, and enable us to enjoy satisfactions
> instead.' (Freud, 1915b, p.280)

Unable to respond adequately to the crisis, institutionalised psychoanalysis seeks a way out by resorting to denial. It refuses to acknowledge or accept the situation. Instead of addressing psychoanalysis as it really is, it decides to stick to the principles which it has hitherto used to manage its association. The result is that a gap arises between what really is and what it wishes were the case. It has been living within this retreat into illusion for years now and thus avoids unpleasure.

The IPA avoids unpleasure by denying the awful writing on the wall, the signs of the decline. The number of its members in the United States has been sinking steadily: the American Psychoanalytical Association accounted for 60 per cent of IPA members in the 1950s, whereas today the figure has fallen to only 33 per cent. The numbers of applicants for psychoanalytical training and the number of candidates undergoing training have also been constantly on the decrease: over the last ten years, there have been 30 per cent fewer applicants to APA institutes. In San Francisco, at the old and renowned APA training institute, there are only four persons on each year of the programme (Annual Report of the Psychoanalytical Institute San Francisco, 1993); between 1980 and 1990, only 68 candidates for training were registered with the total of 36 APA institutes (Cooper, 1990). The situation in Germany also bears mentioning. There, thanks to the new decree governing specialist medical consultants, psychoanalytical training will be shifted away from the institutes, including the DPV, and into the specialist university departments[15]. And in Holland and England the psychoanalytical training institutes have for years been gradually drying up (see van der Leeuw, 1978; Groen-Prakken, 1981 and 1984; Holder, 1984). The drop in the number of medical practitioners is especially sharp and stems from the fact that in almost all countries they can now practise psychotherapy or psychoanalysis without IPA training. In the United States, the number has fallen by 50 per cent (Cooper, 1984). The number of candidates leaving an IPA-approved institute at the end of training without wishing to become IPA members have been on the up, in particular in the United States: at the New York Psychoanalytical Institute, they total some 30 per cent of all candidates. This is also the case in Germany, where the Professional Medical Associations grant doctors the additional title of 'psychoanalyst' even when the applicants do not possess a diploma from a DPV institute. The number of persons who switch from a DPV institute to one at which the entrance requirements are less rigid and lower demands are made as regards training analysis, has grown steadily.

In Germany, teaching professorships for psychotherapy, psychoanalysis and psychosomatic medicine, which until only a few years ago were held mainly by DPV members, are now in part in the hands of representatives of other schools of thought. Wallerstein has observed the same phenomenon in the United States. Psychoanalysts have hardly any chance of being appointed to a chair of psychiatry (Wallerstein, 1991a). Many psychiatric university hospitals offering instruction were once interested in incorporating aspects of psychoanalysis in their training programmes for specialist medical consultants. Today, their place has been taken by behavioural therapy. The loss of prestige psychoanalysis has suffered is evidenced most clearly in psychiatric training for specialist medical consultants in the United States. Whereas in 1970, some 50 to 60 per cent of such programmes consisted of the theory and practice of analytical psychotherapy, the share these account for today is only 2.5 per cent (Wallerstein, 1991a). This is, among other things, attributable to the fact that on completing training, the participants cannot assume that they will be able to earn a living from psychoanalysis. Indeed, 50 per cent of the APA members no longer work as analytical practitioners (Sandler, 1990); they are instead on the payroll at one institution or another. Of the 1,500 psychiatrists completing training in the United States each year, only 109 register for psychoanalytical training at an APA institute (Cooper, 1990). The anti-analytical mood in the United States can also be seen in the fact that the editors responsible did not include symptomatic neuroses and any terminology connected with psychoanalysis in the classification of psychiatric disturbances given in the *Diagnostic and Statistical Manual of Mental Disorders*.

The IPA also avoids discontent by not considering the consequences of the fact that the institutes offer training which is inappropriate in our times. Many of those who complete such training afterwards seek the knowledge provided by additional training outside the domain of the IPA. After all, they face a practical situation in which they are expected to have a knowledge of and experience in procedures which they have not learnt and in which what they have learned (namely, intensive long-term sessions of analysis) tends to be the rare exception. In Germany, for example, as the expert reports compiled by DPV members accompanying applications for funding by patients show, this has led to a mixture of heterogeneous theories and methods, causing confusion in therapeutic work.

The consequences of such denials are an inability to act.

I shall now demonstrate by means of two examples how wide-ranging the illusions are that are necessary to avoid discontent.

The first example:

'An analyst is someone,' writes Sandler, 'who has been trained by our training institutions' (Sandler, 1989). This sentence is only true if two conditions are fulfilled: first of all, that the IPA training institutes still conduct training in line with the IPA principles and, secondly, that the identity of the analyst can still be defined in keeping with Freud's paradigms. I shall show that not all IPA associations fulfil the first condition and that the second has long since ceased to apply. In other words, Sandler's statement denies the profound changes that have occurred and thus avoids unpleasure in this way.

In several countries, IPA training institutions have to offer curricula that only in part (as in the United States; Cooper, 1990) or only just (as in Germany) concur with the IPA's training criteria. Let us take the case of Germany, where quasi-state training regulations define the training institutes' curricula – including those of the DPV institutes. The DPV institutes have to offer the following contents in training, although the IPA states that these are 'foreign to analysis'. *As regards theory*: the psychology of learning, group and family psycho-dynamics, theory and methods for short courses of therapy, psychotherapy, behavioural therapy, group psychotherapy and Balint groups, as well as psychological testing. *As regards practical work*: training in Balint group practice, in hypnosis and autogenic training. Candidates must conduct six courses of psychotherapeutic treatment in line with health insurance guidelines, i.e. courses of low frequency, and totalling 1,000 hours in all, of which one course must be deep psychological psychotherapy, and one short psychotherapy. Moreover, candidates must furnish proof of having led 60 two-hour sessions of ongoing group therapy and having conducted 40 hours of supervision. In other words, above all as regards practical work, it is very difficult to practise the psychoanalytical technique as the IPA understands it. Not only is little time available, but there is also the danger of fusion and confusion. Most candidates therefore only succeed with a great deal of effort in treating two cases 'analytically', and then only manage 300-400 hours in total (Braun, 1992). Anyone who contends that candidates who successfully pass out from such institutions are still analysts in Sandler's sense overlooks that such persons hardly differ from candidates successfully completing analytical training at non IPA-approved institutes – especially since the principle of intensive supervised sessions has fallen victim to IPA prohibition.

Even before this process commenced at the institutes, Edward Joseph, the then IPA President, remarked at the Haslemere Conference in 1976 that the identity of the psychoanalyst could no longer be defined in terms of Freud's paradigms (Joseph, 1979). The conference's concluding communiqué stated that the identity of the analyst cannot be defined unequivocally in terms of the object of research or treatment. Acquiring a specific treatment technique is equally insufficient to establish a psychoanalytical identity: the definition of the social function and role of the analyst culminate in so many contradictions that they do not suffice to determine the analytical identity. In other words, Freud's statement that any work which recognizes the fact that transference and resistance occurs can be applied today to non-analysts, too (Meerwein, 1978, p.42ff.).

What we see here is that the conference reached conclusions on the identity of the analyst which resemble those which I arrived at by perusing the curricula of the training institutes.

Wallerstein's assertion that the difference between analysts of the dissident schools (Silverberg, Radó, Sullivan, Horney) and those in the orthodox psychoanalytical mainstream is smaller than the gap between the mainstream and analysts such as Kohut, Schäfer, George S. Klein, and Peterfreund, who still belong the central IPA massif and thus the orthodoxy (Wallerstein, 1988), also addresses the topic of the analyst's identity[16]. Winnicott is an impressive example here: he breaks the taboo that an analyst must not touch his or her patients (Ferenczi was excommunicated by the IPA for breaching this taboo). When Winnicott states that 'sometimes holding has to be practised physically' (Winnicott, 1974, p.317) he is at greater variance with the central massif than are the representatives of schools of thought outside the IPA who still respect this taboo.

The second example:

Institutionalised psychoanalysis adheres to the following maxim: we can only speak of psychoanalytic practice as such if it consists of five or four sessions a week, is not limited in time, and is not encumbered with provisos foreign to it (e.g. health service stipulations). 'The way the DPV sees itself,' the DPV wrote in 1990, 'is in terms of a course of analysis with highly frequent sessions, both in practice and in training.' This implies for training that training analysis and control cases have to be conducted for at least four hours a week. In 1986, the President of the DPV asserted: 'Anyone rejecting the key importance of the psycho-analytical method – or only accepting it in a reduced form – ceases in essence to be a psychoanalyst' (Appy, 1986). Likewise, in 1991 the President of the IPA, Sandler, stated that the integrity of the psycho-analytical movement was threatened 'because an increasing number of members of the IPA conduct analysis entailing a low attendance fre-quency' (Sandler, 1991, p.1). One consequence of this confusion and these contradictions is, or so Pulver writes in the summary to his survey, that the psychoanalysts who in the United States were already then (1976-7) mainly conducting psychotherapy were having an ever harder time preserving the 'gold' of the analytical transference / counter-trans-ference relationship (Pulver, 1978, p.194). For some years now, this assertion has also applied to most European countries (see below and p.29), in particular to Germany. In respect of the continuation of the 'classical' method as the IPA understands it, this means that there will soon be hardly any lecturers or training analysts who can pass it on. Sandler's 'increasing number' denies the fact that analysts world-wide have always conducted and are predominantly conducting courses of infrequent therapy sessions[17]. Prior to the introduction of psychotherapy paid for by public and private health insurances in Germany in 1967, analysts who were neither training analysts nor prominent members of the community had to earn their living by offering courses of therapy entailing a low attendance frequency which rarely exceeded 300 to 500 hours. Even during times when psychoanalysis was all the rage in the United States and possessed a monopoly on treatment, the number of patients of IPA analysts who between 1952 and 1958 were on long-term courses of psychoanalysis with a high attendance frequency was only 49 per cent (Hamburg, 1947). Only ten years later, Pulver's survey shows that between 1967 and 1978 as many as 70 per cent of patients in psychoanalytical practices were receiving psychotherapy with a low attendance frequency, therapy that was more of a supportive nature and in certain cases was combined with a course of medication (Pulver, 1978). In the same survey, 25 per cent of the members of the APA declared that they were no longer identified with psychoanalysis (meaning the method involving high attendance frequency). Shapiro remarked when assessing the findings of Pulver's survey that only 20 per cent of active APA members still conducted purely psychoanalytical treatment (*ibid*., p.618ff.). Smirnoff found that in France the practice had always been to offer less than four hours a week, even back before 1939 (Smirnoff, quoted in Rotmann, 1988, p.157). In 1987, a statistical inquiry in France confirmed that this situation had not changed: 81 per cent of the analysts who responded to the survey stated that they conducted courses of analysis of only three hours a week (Bergeret et al, 1987).

Champions of analysis defined in terms of the numbers of hours cannot cite Freud in their favour. I need point readers only to the method Freud used for the analysis of the 'Rat Man' (1907) and for Marie Bonaparte[18] in the mid-1920s (Bertin, 1982; see Cremerius, 1990a, p.19).

In countries in which the state healthcare authorities offer psychotherapy or psychoanalysis free of charge (England, Holland), hardly any patients are prepared any longer to embark on long-term courses of analysis involving highly frequent attendance and which they have to finance themselves. As a consequence, hardly anyone applies to undertake training as a psychoanalyst (Holder, 1984; van der Leeuw, 1978; Groen-Prakken 1981, 1984).

The national health authorities and health insurance companies in West Germany have intervened most in the practice and training of the DPV. Since 1990 they have struck analysis with highly frequent attendance from the list of services they offer. In other words, DPV members, who are almost all tied in to the health insurance system, are offering treatment that is not analytical in the DPV sense. It is non-analytical both because infrequent therapy is involved, with the duration of the course restricted to a maximum 240 hours, and because of the stipulations the health insurances make. The practitioners are duty-bound to abide by these stipulations even though, in the view of the IPA, they render analytical therapy as such impossible (Cremerius, 1992a and 1992b).

Freud had far fewer illusions than analysts today. He clearly foresaw the development outlined here and which the IPA so manifestly denies: 'A time will come when there are many analysts but few real courses' (quoted from Morgenthaler, 1965).

Just how strong the denial at work here is can be seen from the fact that institutional psychoanalysis does not even take note of the findings of the 'Menninger Psychotherapy Project', conducted by renowned IPA members. The project was not able to bear out the necessity for attendance being highly frequent. On the contrary, it came to the following conclusion: the proposition that only the classical psycho-analytical method entailing a course featuring highly frequent attendance offers an insight into structural change is untenable. Both, namely insight and structural changes, were discernible in the control group (patients on courses with low-attendance frequency) (Wallerstein, 1986a). Was it not Freud who remarked that psychoanalysis was only 'one [form of therapy] among many' (Freud, 1933a, SE vol. XXII p. 157 and 1926e, SE vol. XX p.248)! It comes as no surprise that the institutional com-munity also denies the findings of another study which has proven that intensive analysis can be damaging: 'it induces the patient's dependency and thus an analysis without end'; Gibeault, 1980).

The following shows in just what abstruse contradictions the IPA embroils itself as a consequence of this denial: A well-known analyst, IPA president at the time, remarked (as quoted above) that the effort made over decades to distinguish psychotherapy from psychoanalysis had borne no fruit (Wallerstein, quoted from Klüwer, 1980, p.21ff.). In this regard, another equally renowned analyst stated, as already indicated, that he suspected 'these considerations were decided more in terms of tactical and political criteria than on a scholarly basis' (Sandler, 1989, p.5). Two years later, the very same Sandler, by then IPA president, claimed: 'If the analytical movement is to survive then we must now do our utmost to maintain the boundaries between analy-tical and non-analytical treatment' (Sandler, 1991, p.1). What is so abstruse about this remark is that in most countries four hours of analysis a week counts as analysis. However, the British Psycho-Analytical Association, of which Sandler is a member, only considers a course of treatment of a minimum of five hours duration per week as analysis. Four hours per week would thus only count as psychotherapy. Sandler, who defended this numerical definition (1991), averred the opposite in 1980 when he defined psychoanalysis as being what an analyst practises, even if he only sees the patient once or twice a week (Klüwer, 1980, p.20).

In view of this situation in the United States and Europe, Parin asked in 1990 whether psychoanalysis, as impaired as it was, even had a due place in today's world or whether it was out of date, a romantic relic like mail coaches, an obsolete Messianic utopia (Parin, 1990, p.4).

The Outlook

Psychoanalysis becomes a normal science

> Psychoanalysis must not be construed as a predeter-
> mined model if it is to be part of reality.

Psychoanalysis as a science only has a future if it consistently continues down the path to becoming a science like any other – it has been going down this path for some years now, albeit slowly and arduously, because its progress has been obstructed by many psychoanalysts. The other precondition for a good future would be that it finds a place where it can go about the immense body of work associated with founding a normal science without being interrupted. It will only be in a position to do so in the form of an 'untrammelled analysis'. And that place must be a public place, a place where Kant's 'reasoning public' is prepared to enter into critical discourse. Regardless of all the objections that can undoubtedly be raised, the university is that place.

What does it mean: psychoanalysis must become a 'normal science'? It means that it has put its early phase, the phase of paradigm formation, of a wealth of daring ideas, of 'the promise of success', as Kuhn called it, behind it and has entered the phase of 'realisation of the promise' (Kuhn, 1972, p.75), namely the 'post-dogmatic age' (Thomä, 1991).

What does this mean for psychoanalysis? What tasks must it now complete in order to realise the promise of early psychoanalytical paradigms? First of all it means doing a lot of clearing-up work! In the stormy early phase, the phase of findings and inventions, of daring hypotheses and of tentative definitions for new concepts, much remained unpolished, unclarified, mere draft. For psychoanalysis to become a normal science, a generation must take on all the work of clearing up the unfinished business. This means a lot of drudgery.

Psychoanalysis represents two fields, namely theory and applied psychoanalysis. The above-mentioned tasks of a normal science have to be accomplished in both fields.

I shall start with the field in which psychoanalysis has been progressing as a normal science for many years now, namely the application of psychoanalysis in the domain of medicine. With the creation of professorships in psychotherapy, psychosomatic medicine and psychoanalysis in West Germany in the early 1960s, psychoanalytical therapy became an object of critical empirical study. Research focuses at present on therapy as process, its effectiveness, and its efficiency. Other areas of research are: comparative methodology (including behavioural therapy, cognitive, systemic and solutions-oriented procedures); the elucidation of diagnostic concepts; experiments with variations on the psychoanalytical method, for example, techniques oriented to patients or situational methods. In other words, we are seeing a return to Freud's technical experiments, for example 'interval technique', and to regain the freedom to decide the medical indications involved, something that Freud postponed as he felt it disturbed the advance of research at the time.

It is also important to promote research in the neglected field of comparative therapy research. What do cognitive, systemic and solutions-oriented methods achieve that the psychoanalytical method does not? And, moreover, what does the psychoanalytical method accomplish when combined with group, body and behavioural therapy, as well as suggestive techniques? The goal here must also be to re-think the old taboo that an analyst is someone who does not touch his patients. Here, in the open domain of the university, the long overdue discussion of Freud's medical case studies is possible. My generation was expected to learn the 'classical' psychoanalytical mode of treatment precisely with regard to them, although they neither concentrated on classical neuroses nor demonstrated classical techniques. Indeed, in the case of the 'Rat man' quite the opposite of the classical technique was presented.

In order to lay the foundations for the scientific justifications for research into therapy, curricula must be expanded far beyond the limits of the contents of IPA training institutes – to include the results of neurophysiology, neuroanatomy, research into the cerebrum, the nerve centres, the two halves of the brain, not to mention knowledge on the early phases of the development of the brain and the medullary sheath, research into twins, etc. Knowledge about the way certain drugs work need to be taught because their use in combination with psychotherapy will be a new field of research.

Psychoanalysis as a theory, as a specific life science, must also advance to the stage of a normal science. This is still, by and large, wishful thinking. The comparatively strong position which research into psychotherapy has attained in medicine to date is still something which psychoanalytical theory needs to achieve. However great the interest in psychoanalysis has always been in certain areas of the humanities (see p. 1 above), it seems to be very difficult to establish independent psychoanalytical teaching and research institutes there.

If I give rein to my 'dreams', then I imagine it as a centre understood primarily as a place of discussion, as a place where everyone interested in psychoanalysis as a science can meet. In order to be able to fulfil this task, the centre would have to unite both research and teaching.

As a teaching institute, it would have to meet Freud's 1926 list of desirable criteria to be fulfilled by a 'psychoanalytical college'. However, it would be superior to the latter in that it would exist in the free, open setting of a university, where what Freud wished for in terms of the curriculum – namely cultural history, mythology, the psychology of religion, and literary studies – are taught by the relevant specialists. It would also be superior in that it would be accessible all day long. And it would naturally also have to teach subjects such as sociology, ethnology, communications theory, the psychology of perception, etc., would promote the neglected field of research into adolescence and periods of life and would, finally, together with empirical researchers, would address topics such as the nature of dreams, sleep, consciousness and unconsciousness, the formation of consciousness and disturbances in consciousness.

The psychoanalytical centre as a location for psychoanalytical training should be open to persons of all fields who were interested in psychoanalytical theory. Freed from the obligation of having to issue a diploma for professional practice, it would be able to devote itself fully to the matter at hand, namely psychoanalysis. In other words, it would also not have to concern itself with training analysis and the supervision of cases of treatment. It could present itself fully as an 'open system' – in Karl Popper's sense. That is to say, it could offer contents from which each person could then choose what they need for their particular purposes, what they feel is best suited to assisting them in the field in which they work or wish to work. It would not require admission procedures and would not assume responsibility for training courses. The real advantage of such training would be that everybody embarking on such a course would become familiar with psychoanalysis as a life science among other life sciences, as 'one truth among others' in the manner in which Eugen Bleuer understood the phrase. At the Sorbonne, such a centre seems to have already been established. For some five or ten years now it has been possible to study for a 'doctorate in psychoanalysis' there.

A research centre would have many tasks to square up to if it wishes to help psychoanalysis become a normal science. And it would have a good chance of tackling them successfully as scientists from numerous fields would be 'right next door' to assist.

Before beginning any sort of specific work, concepts and the creation of concepts would be the first terrain that needs to be cleared up. Despite the magnificent work on a *vocabulary of psychoanalysis*, we still find ourselves walking gingerly across slopes filled with the detritus of random, ambiguous concepts or those which are merely the arcane vocabulary of the initiates. Such clearing up will require the sober approach of researchers schooled in normal science and unafraid of 'sacred cows'.

The other advantage furthering 'normalised' research would be that psychoanalysis could delineate its field of research more precisely than was previously possible in institutional psychoanalysis. There, generalized ideas, general notions on mankind and the world, private philosophies on the meaning of life and of death, of healing, maturity and the true self, that is to say 'ideas in the sense of a cottage industry' (Cooper, 1984, p.255) have led an existence of which the members have often been little aware. The most impressive example for the existence of such vague notions is the presence of unclarified meta-theoretical concepts usually passed on without any reflection and yet located right at the core of psychoanalytical theory formation. The 'Witch meta-psychology' of Freud has not been fully demythologized. Holt speaks of meta-psychology as a wreck that needs to be cleared away in order to gain clear epistemological terrain on which theory formation could commence anew (Holt, 1990). A normal science will not be satisfied with Wallerstein's definition that meta-psychological concepts are metaphors or symbols – namely metaphors with which we live, the articles of our pluralistic, psychoanalytical faith. They function, he claimed, to furnish cohesion for our own inner lack of knowledge (Wallerstein, 1988).

Of paramount importance is the eradication of a rare form of linguistic confusion of tongues: new schools have emerged that deviate from the mainstream but continue to use the terminology of the derivative school. They have imbued these concepts with new meaning, with new semantic content, and the same vocabulary thus now serves two different languages. Finally, and this is a task which presumes a transference-free relationship to Freud, the normal science must dare to work through Freud's paradigms. In this context, questions such as the following will arise: Does a paradigm still fulfil its claim to be more successful in solving a particular problem than the models which compete with it? Does it create a greater approximation of the reality that is hunted for than do the others? Some paradigms need to be rendered more precise, to be expanded, or to be abandoned as untenable.

In this regard, the paradigms also need to be examined to see whether they are historically specific. In other words, we need to ask to what extent they mirror the unreflected trammelling of their creator by the prejudices and values of his day. I am thinking, for example, of Freud's notions on the structure of society, of the role of the father and the family in it, on the woman as a deficient being (penis envy), on the economic conditions and life of that social stratum which back then did not appear in analysts' practices but frequents them today, etc. This critical study of his paradigms will inevitably rely on collaboration with sociologists. That is to say, with scientists who know how to analyse the social reality in which people live today and can show psychoanalysts which structures have changed since Freud first formulated his paradigms.

In conclusion, I would hope in particular that these centres will join forces with representatives of the social sciences and focus intensively on Freud's cultural theory and social criticism, areas that have been neglected for years by the psychoanalytical community. I am convinced that ideas lie waiting here that could help us to arrive at a better understanding of irrational aggressivity and destructivity in society as well as the relations between peoples.

With a view to the next century, I hope that the generation which will then decide the fate of psychoanalysis will not pass it on with missionary zeal, apostolically as the sacrosanct doctrine of the founding fathers, but instead will hand it down as a science which no one can hold a monopoly on, which 'belongs' to all mankind. And I hope that it grasps psychoanalysis as something which must be injected into the never-ending process of science, which never fails to question received knowledge and ever generates knowledge.

I believe that this is how Freud understood psychoanalysis in 1939, the last year of his life, when he once more considered the future prospects of a psychoanalysis, now liberated from the error of the 'psychoanalytical movement', namely the notion that 'We possess the truth'. At the time, Freud stated: 'The validity of psychoanalytic findings is [not] definitely established, while actually they [are] still in their beginning and [need] a great deal of development and repeated verification and confirmation.' (Interview with Peck in Peck, 1940, p.206,).

NOTES

[1] Here, we can discern a tradition dating back to the Old Testament of 'Thou shall be moderate – gather around ye many disciples and build a tower around theory' (*Proverbs*). It is echoed in the history of the 'committee'. Freud made 12 disciples members of the committee and forged an enduring link to them by giving each a ring with an antique Greek intaglio such as he himself wore. His gem was engraved with Zeus' head. In the Gospel according to St. Matthew (9.9 and 10.3) we read that Jesus made Matthew the publican a member of the twelve.

[2] Erikson commented with irony that psychoanalysis had sprung from Freud's mind like 'Athena from Zeus' head.' (Erikson, 1957, p.80).

[3] The value of selection is therefore equivalent to that of random choice: 50 per cent accurate predications, 50 per cent roughly inaccurate predictions, if we tot up the number of candidates who quit during or after training analysis.

[4] In 1918, with the encouragement of Freud, Nunberg submitted a motion at the congress in Budapest that every analyst *should* have undergone analysis himself. Not until 1926 was the motion passed at the Homburg Congress, after some opposition. The concept of 'training analysis' came into existence at that time.

[5] Balint summarized this situation as follows: 'What we see is that the teaching committees and teaching analysts try to keep their esoteric knowledge secret, that they put forward our demands dogmatically, and use authoritarian techniques. On the part of candidates ... we can observe a willing adoption of esoteric legends, and subjection without much protest to dogmatic and authoritarian treatment. We know what goal all these initiation rites have; they are meant to compel the newcomer to identify with the clan. We, by contrast, consciously endeavour to encourage our candidates to develop a strong and critical Ego. Our own behaviour as analysts has traits that run fully at odds to this conscious aim and our training system inevitably leads to a weakening of this Ego function in candidates.' (Balint, 1947, p.317)

[6] The schisms and movements that have prompted groups to split off from the mainstream community range from Jung, Adler, Stekel, Max Graf and Otto Gross through to Melanie Klein, Horney, Radó, Sullivan, Fromm, and Kohut. The schisms have at times truly resembled religious wars, which simply serves to show that we have to do here truly with belief and not with science. I am thinking in particular of the battle between Anna Freud and Melanie Klein, in which both were prepared to resort to any means (cf. Steiner, 1985).

[7] For examples of the hatred of persons undergoing training analysis towards their analysts see Ernest Jones, who throughout his career continually maligned his teaching analyst, Ferenczi: 'A small, cowardly pamphlet maker' (Balint, 1958) who purportedly ended up psychotic (Jones, 1957, p.214). Conversely, teaching analysts have persecuted their analysands. This was the fate of Margaret Mahler. Her teaching analyst, Helene Deutsch, discontinued the analysis and reported to the teaching committee that Mahler was un-analysable (Stepansky, 1989, p.88). This was also the cause for Freud's tragic distantiation from his analysand Ferenczi. For years, he allowed Ferenczi's Wiesbaden lecture to remain unpublished.

[8] In Germany, where admission to provide health-insurance-supported psychotherapy is only granted on the basis of a diploma awarded by a teaching institute approved by the Physicians Federal Association (if one ignores other, difficult means of admission), failure in training leads to admission not being granted.

[9] Secrecy all too easily becomes censorship. As an example, one could cite the first edition of the Fliess letters. The editors failed to mention which passages they had abridged, and included only 168 of 284 letters without stating the principle underlying the selection.

[10] The American Psychoanalytical Association only admitted 'laypersons' to training after being forced to do so by a court ruling – after losing litigation intended to defend the monopoly of medical practitioners. The DPV rescinded its approval of lay analysis when the KBV declared this to not be compatible with the guidelines on psychotherapy.

[11] Just how narrow this makes the scope of the analyst's experience is shown clearly by the fact that many analysts first commence work with the patient if the latter can furnish proof from a bank that he or she has sufficient funds to pay for the entire course of analysis (Kubie, 1956; Menninger, 1958). Swiss analysts who are adherents of the Klein school (to the present day) demand one year's payment in advance.

[12] In Germany, almost all DPV members participate in health-insurance-sponsored psychotherapy schemes – in other words, they have to adhere to their rules (infrequent sessions limited in duration, provision of expert's reports, criteria for economic feasibility and meaningfulness, etc.). As a consequence, the classic form of psychoanalysis as is officially still advocated has been transformed into a form of analytical psychotherapy like any other and is no longer recognized by the IPA as an analytical technique (Cremerius, 1990a, 1992a).

[13] It is noteworthy here that parallel to the emergence of this 'collective motherhood', what Winnicott calls a treatment practice of 'holding' has arisen, i.e. the demand that like a mother the analyst must care for the wellbeing of each patient. It is amazing that this new technique is only considered a variant of the psychoanalytical technique and not viewed in relation to the afore-mentioned changes in society. Again, we see here the social scotoma of institutionalised psychoanalysis.

[14] An example: An IPA Commission was meant to clarify the relationship between psychoanalysis and psychotherapy. After decades of effort (1949 to 1980) it still had not succeeded in finding a definition for the difference on which a consensus could be reached. 'We are,' Wallerstein remarked in this regard in 1980, 'no closer to answering this question after all these years than we were before.' (quoted from Klüwer, 1980, p.21) Sandler states on the same point: 'The efforts to pin-point the difference came to nothing because these important deliberations were conducted more from a tactical and political than from a scholarly viewpoint.' Sandler, 1989, p.5)

[15] The impact the new decree for specialist medical consultants will have on the future of the DPV institutes is already becoming clear. The number of applicants has fallen dramatically – at one of the 14 institutes, only one person is participating in the training programme.

[16] Thomä and Kächele share this opinion: 'The criticism of libido theory and metapsychology presented by Schultz-Hencke at the first Congress of the International Psychoanalytical Association after the war in Zurich would not cause a stir today and many analysts would share it' (Thomä & Kächele, vol. 1, p.12).

[17] 80-year-old Therese Benedek replied to Basch's question as to how many patients she had treated in the strict psychoanalytical sense in the course of her career as follows: probably three or four. Basch added that this concurred with the experiences he and his colleagues had also made (Basch, 1991). Winnicott asserts that the era of such psychoanalysis (the standard method) was invariably nearing its end. And goes on to say: 'of the many patients who come to me … only a very small percentage do in fact get psychoanalytic treatment.'

Just to what extent he in fact deviates from the standard method can be seen from the analysis which Margaret Little undertook with him between 1957 and 1967 (Little, 1991).

[18] At the same time as Freud was treating Marie Bonaparte, Glover was conducting his study on 'The Bases of Therapeutic Results'. His finding: there was neither a substantive nor a formal basis for any talk of a uniform method, a 'core identity' (Glover, 1937).

Helmut Dahmer

The Varying Fortunes of the
'Psychoanalytical Movement'

'The task of the institute, which he wished to call the Freud Institute, was not only to involve acquainting thousands of students with psycho-analytical procedures as a supplement to their medical studies. For the institute was to provide a platform for all of Freud's research interests and to offer the opportunity for students and scholars to become familiar with all the dimensions of his work. It was to be a source of enlightenment for all of those who could not get by in their own particular field without the insights provided by the founder of psychoanalysis. ... But he did not conceal from me his concern that his plans might be thwarted by those among the psychoanalysts who were anti-philo-sophical and, to his mind, anti-Freudian in approach.' Thus reported Max Horkheimer 47 years ago on talks with Ernst Simmel[1] which focused on setting up a psychoanalytical institute in Los Angeles.

The report implies a diagnosis on the state of organised psycho-analysis that has since been confirmed by the direction in which it has developed. Freud's psychology of the unconscious was born from a study of hysteria and dreams, and took its cue from individual biography and cultural history. It was a new version, albeit in a scientific guise, of the *critique of pseudo-nature* which had been developed in German idealism as a philosophy of history with a practical thrust. The assumption was that people do not live directly in a natural environment but instead in a socio-natural lifeworld, shaped by the wishful dreams, the mental productions in which these dreams are enacted, and the struggle of many generations. The world in which they live is history. And the problems of this historical and social world form a 'second nature' which can be neither tackled nor solved by the proven procedures for controlling nature by means of technology. The history of society and the individual biographies embedded in it can neither be explained by analogy with natural processes, nor be interpreted like lucid texts in which intention and expression concur. The history of sociality and of individuals is produced in the *unconscious praxis* of the acting and suffering human beings, who have an inadequate knowledge of the conditions and impact of what they do (or do not do). Precisely for this reason, they certainly regard these conditions and the impact of their actions as 'natural'.

Seen in retrospect, specific invariants of disaster seem to recur constantly in the biography of each individual person and of the collective. At the level of social history, scarcity, inequality and violence – which, despite all the progress made in controlling nature, continue to shape forms of life in even the most advanced societies today – correspond to the traumas we can expect at the level of personal biography. At the end of the 20th century, following Auschwitz and Hiroshima, Kolyma/ Petchora and Cambodia, Uruguay, Argentina, Guatemala and El Salvador, our history can be read primarily as the history of murder. Freud's forecast was that the advancement of society in the framework of those institutions which perpetuated inequality and scarcity would serve to unleash ever greater quantities of uncontrollable aggression among individuals embedded in the masses. His theories and his practical work were geared to nothing less than breaking the repetitive compulsions in personal and cultural history, as these to an ever greater extent ensnare humans in a fateful situation and in the final instance cause them to prefer such conditions to the decline of such a form of life. The discovery of society as pseudo-nature and of anamnesis – of self-reflection as the path to strip that society of its appearance as second nature and to open it for revisions, for the sabotage of man-made fate – was successfully achieved by German idealism on the basis of the experiences gained from the French Revolution.

Marx put this discovery to fruitful use in the late 19th century as regards the dimension of class history and Freud did the same for the dimension of the history of the soul. In the one as in the other, there were more fetishes than facts, as the facts with which we have to do are disguised acts. The agenda of ideology critique is therefore unlike that of the natural sciences and the humanities. It is not interested in proving general hypotheses pertaining to laws, but instead in disempowering compulsions that rest on a lack of awareness among those subjugated to them. It does not focus on the true-to-text appropriation of a meaning passed down in literary documents, but instead on deciphering a counter-meaning that the authors did not themselves understand and which is conveyed as an interlinear version that runs manifestly counter to the traditional meaning. The aim of research here is not to find 'explanations'; these are mere heuristic crutches. The process of research is a process of self-enlightenment conveyed by dialogue, and its goal is an understanding of history and the present, an understanding which spares individuals and society having to search for a safe haven in survival techniques which merely increase their own unhappiness and the misfortune of others.

Under the impression of constantly iterated new historical disasters and ever new triumphs in the technological mastery of nature, the intellectual history of the last hundred years is characterised by the ongoing repression of and discrimination against non-technological modes of changing the world, such as art, and critical revolution. This trend was most clearly expressed in the strategy of the physicalists in the 'Vienna Circle', which upheld the unity of all the sciences[2]. Only those procedures which conformed to a research logic derived from the development of physics were in future to be able to lay claim to the honorary title of 'science'. All the others were to be judged 'nonsense', the verdict reserved for 'metaphysics'. This clearly meant that the problems of the history of life and society were simply excluded from scientific discourse and both spheres left to the 'nonsense' of contemporary ideologues and decisions[3].

In Freud's writings, a psychoanalytical ideology critique appears in the guise of a science; the therapeutic practice of dialogue trades under the name of 'technique'. This label stems on the one hand from Freud's origins in the 'Helmholtz School'[4], and, on the other, is justified by the fact that patients suffering neuroses are subject to a repetitive compulsion as if it were an organic defect, experiencing both as a 'fate' that suddenly overcomes them. Freud's scientific self-understanding and the scientific metaphors he uses in his theory of the soul are rooted in the pseudo-natural character of neurotic sufferings. However, Freud also endeavoured to protect this new science from alien elements at home, from the 'doctors' and the 'priests', above all from the scientistically oriented medical scientists and psychologists, not to mention the apostles of (religious or political) illusion. The fear that psychoanalysis might fall into the hands of the human engineers and seducers of the masses prompted Freud to dedicate it to 'a profession of secular psychologists who need not be doctors and must not be priests'[5]. Yet organised psychoanalysis has marched down precisely the path which

Freud warned against, namely that which leads to its subsumption under medicine; it was the path of least resistance, of the greatest social prestige, and the surest income. The conflation of psychoanalytical ideology critique and a 'natural science of the soul', i.e. a flirtation with the physicalist agenda, has made the psychoanalysts susceptible to the illusions of scientism. The critique of religion as up-dated by Freud was, by contrast, better equipped to facing other doctrines of salvation; for this reason, gurus had no chance in the International Association.

The 'talking cure' is unmistakably the late product of a liberal era characterised by competitive capitalism. Freud's Ego theory was modelled on the way educated citizens subject to no economic and political worries could live – although their relative economic and emotional autonomy was already under threat. The malaise of this long-dominant social stratum was the theme of the literature contemporaneous with it, from Schnitzler to Musil. Before the liberal, cultured citizens were pushed aside by the trust magnates and the hordes of clerks in the 20th century, they had institutionalised the instructions on self-reflection as a service – one of the most valuable of their legacies.

The first and second generation of Freudian researchers studying the workings of the soul were German Jewish intellectuals, men with a cosmopolitan outlook, indebted to the 'God Logos', freelancers without inheritances, medics with a cultural-revolutionary mission, freethinkers and bohemians, scholars without professorships, social scientists and philanthropists, revolutionaries and utopians. Socially, they were tied to the affluent middle class, whilst exposing the lies on which the lives of its members rested, and were despised and discriminated against by established doctors and psychologists alike. Politically, they were liberal in inclination or well-disposed to the workers movement, although the intellectuals and functionaries did not like them much. They took to the trenches against the Church, the authoritarian state, and repressive culture and were therefore cursed as 'disruptive', 'decadent' and 'anarchist'. In other words, the specialists in twisted biographies, 'Ego weaknesses' and autoplasticity fell between all stools.

The social and intellectual history of the psychoanalytical movement has still to be written. However, the general character of its development over the last few decades is clearly discernible. Psychoanalysis' false self-conception as a natural science, its conscious neglect of sociology and political abstinence – all these were to be found in Freud's thought. And what helped such trends win out at the cost of others was the shock the majority of the psychoanalysts felt in light of their expulsion from their Central European mother culture and the transplantation of psychoanalysis into the Anglo-American cultures in which they sought refuge. Thus, the victory of the Nazis in Germany and the subsequent subjugation of most of Europe by Hitler's armies not only extinguished the German workers movement as a revolutionary force but also wiped out the psychoanalytical movement as an agency of cultural revolution.

The Nazi mass movement, inimical as it was towards the masses, was a rebellion exploited by the real captains of German industry, a rebellion by all those whose hopes had been dashed by developments in Germany after the First World War and who had not shared in the privileges of bourgeois society. And the Nazis crushed the workers movement, which could have endangered finance capital and prevented the war and the Holocaust. They also destroyed the preserves of urban intellectual culture which had been protected by institutional power from below and from the outside world, even if that culture had not possessed any power itself. It had, rather, constituted a sphere of free discourse, of untrammelled domestic discussion, of therapeutic dialogue free from censure, of scientific disputes and parliamentary debate. Despite the experience of the First World War and the social struggles that followed it, and despite Freud's recognition of the precarious status of contemporary civilisation, the majority of the psychoanalysts were not able to realise that the establishment of a fascist dictatorship would bring with it the destruction of their own lifeworld[6].The illusion that psychoanalysis could, in however reduced a form, survive as an *institution* under the racist reign of terror[7] – and some non-Jewish psychoanalysts continued to nurture it years after the Nazis had seized power – attests to such a blindness toward reality. Let us recall the traumatic insight that in times of social crisis the majority does not respect the socially-conceded domain for reflection and critique (in which the psychoanalytical movement, like any other liberal and radical reform movement, exists); instead, the entire domain is liquidated by the classes and groups engaged in combat. Paradoxically, it stripped the majority of psychoanalysts (and other groups of intellectuals, too) of the courage and ability to see beyond the horizons of the prevailing social *status quo* and perceive those trends which go beyond it – for better or for worse. This is the reason for their disinclination to take a stance on 'burning issues of the day'[8], and for their anti-'communist' pro-capitalism. And the persecution did not stop after the end of the Third Reich! In the Soviet Union and states affiliated with it, organised psychoanalysis was not tolerated. In the countries of South and Latin America, where the position of the ruling class was shored up by the influence of the United States in the form of torture and massacres, psychoanalysts are also often included on the black lists of the death squads (in Argentina, for example).

Since the 1930s, having initially aggressively brought its influence to bear in the most different areas of the humanities as well as in the social and natural sciences, psychoanalysis has been on the retreat. The psychoanalysts succeeded in becoming naturalised citizens in the countries to which they had emigrated. The price they paid, was, however, high. Catapulted out of a culture which had spawned not only victorious positivism but also critical theories, the Freudians tried to adapt their own theory of man and culture (influenced by Schelling, Schopenhauer, and Nietzsche) to the empiricism and pragmatism of the Anglo-American world. However, unlike the 'Vienna Circle', Freud's Viennese School was now on foreign soil. A traumatised generation of psychoanalysts, their high-flying hopes dashed, tried hard to mimic the university medicine and psychology practised in their host countries. They limited themselves to therapy, to a psychology of the Ego and self, to problems of family socialisation. And in so doing they earned the respect of psychologists of personality and micro-sociologists, indeed even of theologians.

The tolerance psychoanalysis has since enjoyed was bought by means of autotomy. It is a repressive tolerance, for its tacit precondition is the marginalisation and obliteration of those two intercommunicating vibrant centres of Freud's theory, namely the doctrine of drives and of culture. (Not to forget that these two centres were the reason for the fascination of psychoanalysis, and the initial scandal it caused.) 'It is,' Max Horkheimer wrote in 1939, 'as if the intellectuals who have been driven into exile have been robbed not only of their civil rights, but also of their minds. Thought, the only mode of behaviour which would stand them well, has been discredited. The "Jewish-Hegelian" jargon .. is now considered completely over the top. Breathing a sigh of relief, they throw this uncomfortable weapon away...'[9]

In this way, psychoanalysis in emigration shed its cultural-revolutionary content [10]. An intimidated psychoanalysis is not just a reduced psychoanalysis but one without substance and guts.

Decades later, toward the end of the 1960s, the unease about the deficiencies of psychoanalysis became manifest. The leadership of the American Psychoanalytical Association formed a committee of investigation with the following brief: 'to ascertain why there was a lack of new psychoanalytical insights in central areas of analytical knowledge'[11]. The commission recommended changing the recruiting system as well as specialisation among psychoanalysts and institutes to ensure a division of labour. However, this had little chance of making any impact, as, to quote Paul Parin:

'The function of the psychoanalytical associations and the training institutes that are dependent on them focuses ever more clearly on eliminating all persons [i.e. persons leading an existence on the margins of mainstream psychoanalysis] who do not conform with the established social caste [of psychoanalysts] and on imparting an ever more comprehensive specialist knowledge in terms of both theory and practice while excluding everything which could be termed the emancipatory mission of psychoanalysis.'[12]

Candidates for training have to subject themselves to 'what is now the quite extensive ritual of the institutes and a highly institutionalised professional guild. They' need to 'have devoted 10-12 years of their life to medical and psychiatric training (each with its own special selection criteria, and these are at loggerheads with the requirements for analysis).'[13] In 1959, Anna Freud summarised the development of psychoanalysis when she remarked 'that those rebellious and profoundly inquisitive minds in the first generation who carried the psychoanalytical movement forward; they were followed by another which consisted of conformist administrators and multipliers of the *status quo*.'[14] This trend is no doubt not irreversible, but it certainly cannot be corrected simply by greater differentiation and by supplementing the existing psychoanalytical institutions.

The face of international psychoanalysis has been decisively shaped since 1945 by its new, North American hub, even in areas where relics of pre-War psychoanalytical culture persisted and non-conformists such as Mitscherlich, Lacan or Parin developed alternatives to mainstream psychoanalysis. And even the psychoanalysis which re-emerged in post-War West Germany continues to represent the defeated, intimidated version of psychoanalysis. Despite Mitscherlich's efforts, psychoanalysis is handed down in a semi-truncated form; despite Richter's efforts, the normal analyst remains politically abstinent; despite Parin's efforts, the analyst today hardly looks beyond the confines of his professional work and his own culture. 'The psychoanalyst of today is ... no "citoyen"..., but has instead become a West German citizen who has withdrawn into a social niche in order to be able to go about his interruption-prone psychoanalytical practice in peace and quiet and be spared the travail of political events,' wrote one Frankfurt psychoanalyst of his colleagues[15]. This intimidated psychoanalysis hardly attracts non-conformists, heretics or seekers of the truth willing to take risks; the opposite is the case: it tends to produce somewhat timid, apolitical therapists who are admittedly well endowed with all the status symbols of the upper middle class.

The image of the profession which those who are deciding whether or not to undergo additional training in order to become psychoanalysts have in mind is that of a specialist doctor, not of a seeker and dis-seminator of unpleasant truths. Invariably, the customs of the normal analyst today and the doctrine to which such analysts orient themselves contradict each other. How can someone who shuts himself off from so much reality be expected to provide enlightenment? How can someone who leads so quietist a life be critical? How can a Freudian love of truth, lack of prejudice and non-conformism[16], how can a materialist-atheistic theory of man and culture (in the light of which the current establishment in which we live shows itself to be deficient and in need of change) be compatible with a lifestyle of which a dentist would be proud? Many of Freud's adepts today are not up to handling Freud as a role model, let alone the section of his doctrine not used professionally, and this results in the swift spread of an unhappy consciousness among their number. The interest of specialists and intellectuals in psycho-analysis has contracted to the same degree that the interest among psychoanalysts in political issues and in developments in the other life and human sciences has shrunk. Psychoanalysis is no longer considered provocative – instead, it is regarded quite simply as irrelevant. The new tolerance shown to psychoanalysis stems mainly from indifference. Those that praise it often do not know what they are talking about. And the esteem now accorded psychoanalysis in the self-limited guise it has given itself is often mistaken for a 'victory' of Freudian enlight-enment – something which has certainly not yet been remotely achieved. Against the background of discrimination and persecution, the at times quite luxuriously furnished ghetto in which psychoanalysis exists today can be mistaken for a 'position of power'[17]. However, the reduced ability to duel with other sciences, and the political quietism of psychoanalysis' disciples make it even more defenceless than it was in the days of the pioneers. Who will defend psychoanalysis when it again falls into social disgrace? Who will stand up for it then?

Given these conditions, what we need today is a Psychoanalytical Research Institute which makes the *inner clarification of psychoanalysis* its main task and delegates treatment, outreach care, and training (in a modern way) to existing institutions. For everything which is well or for that matter poorly provided by the activities of existing institutions is without doubt 'important'. However, the future of psychoanalysis depends on clarifying precisely those issues excluded by such activities. A critical awareness needs to be created of the fate of psychoanalysis to date, namely its history of intimidation and reactive self-mutilation, if we are to break the bane and the disconsolate consciousness of psychoanalysts is to be enlightened.

The first task facing a research institute dedicated to bringing about a 'turnaround' in the development of psychoanalysis would be to write the twofold history of the psychoanalytical movement and psy-choanalytical theories. Exposing the way in which the successive psychoanalytical theories and schools depended on contemporary philosophies[18], reconstructing and contextualising the linkage between psychoanalytical theory formation and organisational form in terms of general socio-cultural and political developments – all of this will require a far-reaching revision of the relationship of psychoanalysts with sociology and historiography on the one hand, and with philosophy as well as a theory of language, on the other. Indeed, the relationship between psychoanalysis and politics – and it was problematic from the outset and, once psychoanalysis had been driven into exile, became disturbed – would need to be revised as part of creating a clearer view of the history of our own 'movement'. A psychoanalyst who today recollects, for example, the range of ways his colleagues in the 1930s actually behaved towards the Nazi regime will not be able to avoid asking what was 'right' or 'wrong' back then, and will also have to ask whether his own political approach is compatible with his judgement on the political stance among psychoanalysts back then[19].

The preconditions for writing the history of psychoanalysis include the (long overdue) elaboration of a historical and critical edition of Freud's collected works, including his pre-psychoanalytical writings and letters. An edition of *The Interpretation of Dreams* could act as the model here: it would document the history of the text, as well as the changes and extensions made to it in the course of the various editions, and provide commentaries, thus shedding light on the relationship with competing theories of dream interpretation and to Freud's oeuvre as whole. In conjunction with preparatory work for a history of the psychoanalytical movement, it is high time we also had a reliable bibliographical lexicon of psychoanalysts that gives outlines of their lives, what happened to them, and what they taught. These tasks can only be carried out if public interest in the subject is kindled, if sufficient financing is found, and a staff of qualified historians, archivists, Germanists, etc. is recruited.

A second area to be covered by our proposed Psychoanalytical Research Institute would be to eliminate the privileged access of doctors and psychologists to psychoanalytical training. The commission whose work Heinz Kohut commented upon above already asked 'whether it could not be that analysts with a non-medical training – for example, teachers, educationalists, members of the clergy, artists, philosophers, philologists, lawyers, historians, art historians, etc. – could not strongly stimulate psychoanalytical research prompting it to embark in new directions, which it so seems to shy from most recently.[20]' Nothing would do more to boost new ideas, interdisciplinary dialogue and the spread of psychoanalytical findings than the admission to training analysis of post-graduate students from the humanities and social sciences who do *not* want to become psychotherapists.

A research institute for psychoanalysis should, moreover, conduct a pilot project on 'training analysis for non-therapists' and delegate this task to suitable training institutes. 'But anyone who has passed through such a course of instruction, who has been analysed himself, who has mastered what can be taught today of the psychology of the unconscious, who is at home in the science of sexual life, who has learnt the delicate technique of psycho-analysis, the art of interpretation, of fighting resistances, and of handling the transference – anyone who has accomplished all this *is no longer a layman in the field of psycho-analysis*. He is capable of undertaking the treatment of neurotic disorders'[21]– and will nevertheless not earn his living as a 'lay analyst' (that is, as a non-medical therapist).

Thirdly, the Psychoanalytical Research Institute such as we need today would have to include in its canon the now-forgotten art of presenting therapies in the form of case studies. Only in case studies such as those Freud wrote can the unique experience which psychoanalysts make with their patients be given objective form and communicated in such a way that it can be incorporated into a theory of our current epoch. In this context, psychoanalysts could follow in the tracks of Siegfried Bernfeld and Alfred Lorenzer and start thinking the independent logic of their own therapeutic procedure (i.e. without holding on to the existing research logics of the natural sciences and the humanities as if they were the be-all and end-all of research). To date, they have, with differing degrees of success, simply delegated this task to philosophers bereft of psychoanalytical experiences. This would be an important step towards re-creating the field's ability to joust with the other sciences, towards generating an argumentative psychoanalysis worth its salt. Psychoanalysts who focused on epistemology and on how that science should present its work would, following in the footsteps of Otto Fenichel and Paul Parin, soon abandon any naive psychologism. Indeed, they would learn that the *social* significance of biographies can only be recognised against the background of an adequate notion of the structure and developmental trends of current society, that the logic of society's development cannot be reduced to psychology, and that the 'sociological way of thinking' presumes a specialist training quite comparable with the acquisition of a psychoanalytical ear.

Fourthly, the research institute I am outlining here would work towards systematically expanding the shrunken circle of psychoanalysts' interests[22]. It would prepare the Renaissance of 'Freudian philosophy' after decades during which the Freudian theory of drives and culture has been advanced by non-analytical philosophers (such as Georges Bataille and Herbert Marcuse) or by lone wolves and outsiders to the guild (such as Alexander Mitscherlich). Were the work on the topics addressed in the *Three Essays on the Theory of Sexuality* and *Civilization and Its Discontents* to be continued, then we might finally uncover what the change in cultural sexual morality (the *isolation* of sexuality under the guise of 'liberalisation') really means for the emotional worlds of our contemporaries and how they endeavour by *scotomisation* to escape the *horrors* of a civilisation to which they are exposed by dint of the risk of nuclear war.

Such a research institute would swiftly become a centre for devising and disseminating irritating but liberating insights. Its staff would no longer view apolitical therapists as their ideal, but instead would (fifthly) kindle the public debate on those taboo issues which must be cleared up if democracy is to have a future and as a collective we are to survive. They would use Freudian ideology as a critique to cultivate political discussions and these will become all the more fierce in the years of crisis that lie ahead. A psychoanalysis represented by such a research institute would break out of its armoured existence and would again square up to the task of using the means at its disposal to fight to achieve 'a state of things in which life will become tolerable for everyone and civilisation no longer oppressive to anyone.[23]'   (1983)

II

I have attributed the standstill which the 'psychoanalytical movement' came to decades ago and the peace the majority-psychoanalysts made with civilisation while transforming Freudian critique into a psycho-technique, on the one hand to the 'scientification' (positivisation) of Freudian psychology by 'mandarins' such as Heinz Hartmann and, on the other, to the violent expulsion of the majority-psychoanalysts from their training centres in Berlin and Vienna. Discrimination and per-secution caused the Freudian doctors and psychologists in the 1920sand 1930s to seek their salvation by neutralising the Freudian Enlightenment and deserting the ranks of the 'nay-sayers', as Siegfried Bernfeld called them. This history of the psychoanalytical community has given rise to those strange methods of selection, training and discourse practised by the Freudian guild today, methods which now count as guarantees of 'orthodoxy'. And this history has shaped the characteristic, priest-like and timid stance of today's psychoanalytical doctors of the soul. They shed no tears over the decline of the 'psychoanalytical movement' and the reduction of Freudian philosophy to therapy. For it is precisely this history which they have to thank for what they appreciate most: an untroubled and comfortable existence. The project of making the psy-choanalytical practitioners aware of the decline and fall of the 'psycho-analytical movement' with the assistance of a 'research institute', of which Freud dreamed, and then perhaps, with their help revise things, is, in itself, utopian ...

Over the last ten years, the Frankfurt Sigmund Freud Institute has still not become a 'centre for devising and disseminating uncomfortable but liberating insights'. And the psychoanalysts have presented them-selves to their contemporaries more in the guise of hermits, moral preachers and union functionaries than as people who resist the super-stitions of their age while rendering the course of cultural developments comprehensible for themselves and others, struggling to combat the threat of pending barbarism. A historical and critical collected works of Freud has yet to be produced, and 'piety' continues to block the complete, that is to say uncensored publication of his correspondence (with Martha Bernays or Arnold Zweig). 'Piety' also influences the way the history of the organisation is treated, even though the latter now flourishes in antiquarian form. Over half a century after the expul-sion of Wilhelm Reich from the Psychoanalytical Association (in 1934), there are those who still deny that this expulsion even took place ...

'Lay-analysis' has not been rehabilitated, let alone institutionalised. Any theories of the instincts and of civilisation have been suspended and what Adorno termed a 'brooding psychologism' acts as if Otto Fenichel had never put pen to paper.

The fate of Freudian Enlightenment fatally resembles that of Marxian critique. The critique of the capitalist economy was transformed first by reformist social democrats into a 'world view' and then by terroristic Stalinists into a 'state religion'. The guild's administrators in charge of the Freudian tradition first gave the Freudian critique of civilisation and the psyche 'a scientific basis', and then forgot about it. While Freud, like Nietzsche and Mach before him, had recognised that the autonomous Ego was 'not to be saved' and therefore 'knew of no consolation', decades later therapists who cite him try to give confused souls a lift with 'oceanic feelings'. Any hopes are illusory that this trend might be revised by the psychoanalysts themselves, and today they are organised in professional associations which are at the same time communities sharing the same world view. The timetables of such organisations only include one-way streets. For this reason, they can adjust to match changing conditions, but not avert them. Their supporters live under the spell of traditions they have not shed light on. For this reason, the psychoanalytical 'movement' today is as dead as its Marxian counterpart.

The social catastrophes of our century that have not yet been understood will become the nightmare of the next century. New generations will try to find a way out of the labyrinth of culture. And they will seek counsel from the great puzzle-solvers of the 19th and early 20th centuries, and will not heed the turnkeys who locked liberating thoughts away in their own systems of prison-houses. The 'psychoanalytical movement' is history. Freudian Enlightenment, by contrast, will continue to inspire many a twilight of the idols and a social revolution.

NOTES

[1] Max Horkheimer, "Ernst Simmel und die Freudsche Philosophie," (1948) in: B. Görlich et al, *Der Stachel Freud. Beiträge und Dokument zur Kulturismus-Kritik*, (Frankfurt/Main, 1980), pp.139-48; here, p.145f. (Also in Horkheimer, *Gesammelte Schriften*, vol. 5, [Frankfurt/Main, 1987], pp.396-405; here, p.403f.).

[2] See Victor Kraft, *Der Wiener Kreis. Der Ursprung des Neopositivismus*, (Vienna, 1950), 2nd expanded ed., (Vienna, 1968). Hubert Schleichert (ed.), *Logischer Empirismus. Der Wiener Kreis* (Munich, 1975).

[3] See Max Horkheimer, 'Der neueste Angriff auf die Metaphysik' (1937), in: *Gesammelte Schriften*, vol. 4, (Frankfurt/Main, 1988), pp. 109-61.

[4] See Siegfried Bernfeld, 'Freuds früheste Theorien und die Helmholtz-Schule' (1944), in: S. Bernfeld & S. Cassirer Bernfeld, *Bausteine der Freud-Biograpik*, ed. by I. Grubrich-Simitis, (Frankfurt/Main, 1981), pp.54-77.

[5] Letter to Oskar Pfister of November 25, 1928. In: Freud & Pfister, *Briefe 1909-1939*, ed. E. L. Freud & H. Meng, (Frankfurt/Main, 1963), p.136.

[6] "Liberalism contained the necessary elements for a better society. Law was still universal and applied to the rulers, too. The state was not yet directly their instrument. Anyone who expressed an independent opinion was not necessarily lost. Admittedly, such protection existed only in a small part of the earth, in the countries to whom the others were in thrall. Even this unsteady justice was limited to partial geographic areas. Yet anyone who was part of a restricted human order should not be surprised if he is occasionally subject to its restrictions." Max Horkheimer, 'Die Juden und Europa,' (1939) in: *Gesammelte Schriften*, vol. 4, (Frankfurt/Main, 1988), pp.308-31.

[7] See on this, among others, the essays by Lohmann, Rosenkötter, Brainin and Kaminer in: Hans-Martin Lohmann (ed.), *Psychoanalyse und Nationalsozialismus. Beiträge zur Bearbeitung eines unbewältigten Traumas*, (Frankfurt/Main, 1984).

[8] See Paul Parin, 'Warum die Psychoanalytiker so ungern zu brennenden Zeitproblemen Stellung nehmen. Eine ethnologische Betrachtung,' (1978) in: Helmut Dahmer (ed.), *Analytische Sozialpsychologie*, (Frankfurt/Main, 1980), vol. 2, pp.647-62.

[9] Horkheimer, 'Die Juden und Europa,' op cit, p.115.

[10] The Surrealists, protagonists of the cultural revolt between the wars, rightly considered Freud a comrade-in-arms in the battle against a culture which culminated in as yet unknown barbarism, in unbelievable terror.

[11] Heinz Kohut, 'Forschung in der Amerikanischen Psychoanalytischen Vereinigung. Ein memorandum,' in: *Psyche*, 25 (1971), pp.738-57, here p.740.

[12] Parin, 'Warum die Psychoanalytiker', op. cit., p.655.

[13] *Ibid*

[14] Reported by Parin, op. cit., p.655.

[15] Wolfram Lüders, 'Psychoanalyse versus Familientherapie,' in *Psyche*, 37 (1983), pp. 462-9.

[16] This is expressed in a characteristic letter from Freud to Ernst Simmel (of July 1, 1927): 'You should, at least, not devote so much effort to convincing people who do not wish to be convinced, and should not give the impression that you wish it... We should surely uphold the principle of not compromising with those from whom we can expect nothing, but who stand to gain everything from us.' Quoted from Horkheimer, *Ernst Simmel und die Freudsche Philosophie,* op. cit., (Note 1.), p.147 *Gesammelte Schrifte*, vol. 5, p.405).

[17] 'Psychoanalysis, initially combated and scorned, and then ostracized and persecuted in its Austro-German mother country, has since become an ideological world power,' wrote D. E. Zimmer in his *'Dossier': 'Der Aberglaube des Jahrhunderts'*, in: *Die Zeit*, 45, Nov. 5,

1982, p.17. This corresponds to a report on a DPV conference in Wiesbaden (K.A., 'Der langsame Fortschritt,' in: *Frankfurter Allgemeine Zeitung*, Nov. 13, 1982, p.27): 'Instead of pride, we could hear worry behind Dieter Ohlmeier's remarks that the German Psycho-analytical Association which he leads was "in all respects armed with power and influence".'

[18] See, as an example of such a critical history of ideas, the essays by Rudolf Heinz on the question of *Psychoanalyse und Kantianismus*, (Würzburg, 1981).

[19] See on this point the essays in the volume edited by H. M. Lohmann, *op. cit.*, (Note 7, above).

[20] Kohut, 'Forschung in der Amerikanischen...', op. cit., p.743.

[21] Sigmund Freud, *The Question of Lay-Analysis*, in: *Two Short Acounts of Psycho-Analysis*, SE vol. XX, p. 228.

[22] 'On the other hand, analytic instruction would include branches of knowledge which are remote from medicine and which the doctor does not come across in his practice: the history of civilization, mythology, the psychology of religion and the science of literature. Unless he is well at home in these subjects, an analyst can make nothing of a large amount of his material.' (Freud, *The Question of Lay-Analysis*). Today, we would need to expand Freud's curriculum to include social history, contemporary history, a theory of language. and ethnology...

[23] Sigmund Freud, *The Future of an Illusion* (1927), SE vol. XXI, p.50.

Ludger Lütkehaus

The Past of Psychoanalysis

Anyone who has inhabited a particular discipline for quite a long time and has often tried to discover what its origins were, may sometimes feel tempted to ask what further fate lies before it. But you will soon find that the value of such an inquiry is diminished from the outset by several factors. Above all, because there are only a few people who can survey human activity in its full compass. Indeed, the less a man knows about the past, the more insecure his judgement of the future must prove to be. And there is the further difficulty that in a judgement of this kind the subjective expectations of the individual play a part which it is difficult to assess; and these turn out to depend on purely personal factors in his own experience, on the greater or lesser optimism of his attitude to life. Finally, there is the the curious fact that in general people experience their present naïvely; they have first to put themselves at a distance from it – the present, that is to say, must have become the past – before it can yield vantage points from which to judge the future.

Thus anyone who gives way to the temptation to deliver an opinion on the probable future of our discipline will do well to remember the difficulties I have just mentioned, as well as to bear in mind the un- certainty that attaches quite generally to any prophecy. It follows from this, as far as I am concerned, that I shall beat a hasty retreat in the face of a task that is too great, and shall promptly seek out the small tract of territory which has claimed my attention hitherto … .

It was without doubt a wise decision, just as the author of these lines cannot be denied exhibiting caution, circumspection and even a degree of ponderous slowness. You will have noticed the absence of quotation marks. With a few elisions and adaptations I have appropriated through citation that text which must inevitably be quoted in any consideration of the future of psychoanalysis, namely Freud's *The Future of an Illusion*. I have naturally not done so in an absurd bout of megalomania, such as even an essay-writing amateur in matters of psychology could not be excused. Instead, I have chosen to do so because the text elaborates on significant matters as regards any form of prognosis and highlights symptomatic issues for the topic of 'Freud, psychoanalysis, and the future'. For all the author's unhealthy veneration of Freud, the topic is often not pleasant.

1. Only in two of Freud's writings (German publication dates: 1910; 1927) does the word 'future' appear in the title. His pioneering work, with which he heralded the century of psychoanalysis, namely the *Interpretation of Dreams*, can be grasped as a reduction of a psychological dimension hitherto held mainly to be prophetic or prospective. And the type of wish fulfilment Freud analyses in the *Future of an Illusion* seems to be related only to the future. In truth, however, it is a monument to a past that the soul has not yet overcome. In short, psychoanalysis is in essence a science of the past; it interprets both present and future as defined by the past.

We should therefore believe Freud when he states, and he says it twice, that he gave in to 'temptation' with his forecast. He immediately reins himself in epistemologically speaking, referring to the limitation of personal insights which are all the greater as regards the question of the future, the less you know about the past and present; and with regard to the subjective factor, including a 'greater or lesser' (the present author, as the reader will soon see, tends to the 'lesser') 'principle of hope'. Finally, there is the naive lack of distance humans show towards the present, which only becomes suitable in terms of knowledge for 'judging the future' when invested with the blessing of the past tense. All of this relativises any approximation of the 'probable future', however much this, and to this extent to a certain degree prophetically, is defined as 'fate'.

At any rate, we have the pleasure of hearing Freud publicly succumbing to temptation. Yet his prediction for the future of psychoanalysis, based on trust in the subdued but stubborn 'voice of the intellect' is moderately confident yet decidedly negative as regards religious illusion. Psychoanalysis has a real future: Freud in the somewhat unaccustomed role of the cautious optimist. Religion is without a future: Freud in the customary role of enlightening disillusioner. Religion is carefully not labelled bluntly as an 'error' (even though Freud on occasion allows his readers to see that religion entails a denial of reality). Indeed, the character of religion is something as desirable as wish fulfilment is, quite apart from any question of the truth of religion. And precisely this is what prompts its definition as illusion.

In view of this, a disciple such as Oskar Pfister, who was as true to psychoanalysis as he was to religion, was not able to suppress his rejoinder: 'The illusion of a future' (1928). This inversion is naturally not free of well-believing Christian revanchism. Vicar Pfister understandably does not wish to believe in the 'prophesy of a religion-less future' (p.149). He responds with a dual strategy which corresponds to his double bonds. Firstly, he exposed the scientism in Freud's paradox 'belief in science as the source of human happiness' (p.170), showing it to be an *ersatz* for religion and a wish-fulfilling illusion. In the same breath he functions as theologian and acts the Baptist. Freud the purported atheist found himself unintentionally 'not far from the realm of God', indeed close to 'the Lord's throne' – definitely a surprising place to be. What had Freud done? Nothing other than combating 'religion as religion' (p.150). We all know the 'for he was one of us' syndrome, the missionary method of making the enemy one of our community. Perhaps we need simply to ignore Pfister's value judgements and intentions, but not his diagnosis as such, in order to arrive at an authentic analysis. Can one be as sure as Freud was that psychoanalysis is not an illusion? And all the talk of its future – is it actually anything more than the wish-fulfilling illusion of the future of an illusion? Why juxtapose the various illusions, psychoanalysis and religion, to each other in this manner? Has not psychoanalysis at least achieved the status of a high church, an institutionalised Church complete with dogma and hierarchy and the obligatory sects – as is often the case with churches – not completely disinclined to adopt the more subtler forms of indoctrination and psychological terror?

Here and there, psychoanalysis continues to understand itself as part of that impressive cultural and social liberation movement which termed itself 'Enlightenment', to use a label at which the post-moderns (in equal measure snobbish and corrupt), so strongly turn their noses up. Both share a central thrust, emphatically voiced by Freud's impious and joyful message of the illusionary future of the religious illusion. Both stand under the sign of critique. Both are geared to autonomy as a yardstick. Both are at heart disillusioning. Enlightenment started as a critique of idols and reached its late climax in Freud's critique of illusions – and this is the inextricable link between the two as long as the psychopathology of contemporary life has not completely overwhelmed a memory of history: 'psycho-analytic enlightenment' (Freud, 1910, p.114, and frequently elsewhere) is a synonym.

Disillusionment is clearly a force (and, for all the reality principle, also entails profound intellectual enjoyment) which cannot be dropped at will or even paralysed. So why should it shy away from anything? It thus rebounds against the intellectual movements which operate in its name. And it gives itself the agenda of 'enlightening the enlighteners', 'disillusioning the disillusioners', i.e. the disillusioners' illusions, and potentially this includes the people themselves.

Those elements of psychoanalysis that are neither enlightened nor Enlightenment cannot escape such disillusionment. And these by no means include just late counter-enlightenment distorted histories and regressions, but also evidently pre-Enlightenment residues, the hereditary scripts of an unredeemed past. Analysis of analysis requires more than just the analysis of analysts, which the institution of 'training analysis' (a contradiction in itself) already conducts so integratively – instead of breaking institutional chains. In a nutshell: here the topic becomes psychoanalysis as an illusion, or, to point it up, the issue is psychoanalysis as the illusion of Enlightenment and disillusion. And the question as to its future is raised as the question as to the future of an illusion. That is to say, to the extent that this future itself is an illusion, the question is that of the illusion of a future of an illusion.

By virtue of its self-critical masochism – and this is surely a constitutive strand of any enlightening disillusionism – such an approach also insists on asking what future it *itself* still has. It is probably also an illusion that it has a future. But one cannot be thorough enough when such issues are involved. At the end of the day, the illusion of the future of psychoanalysis is only a segment of the future *as* illusion.

Clearly, Pfister's formulation has ramifications that go further than he himself intended. One only needs be as brash as only an essay-writing dilettante such as the one cited above can risk being: happy to pin his colours to a mast, ready to be programmatical, always glad to offer a declaration of principles. It is therefore all the more advisable to bear Pfister's self-limiting remarks in mind: The object cannot be to don the 'prophet's cloak' (1928, p.150). It is good to remain content with the role of meteorologist. It is meteorologists who often give clouds a silver lining, or alternatively paint a bleak outlook of things. Moreover, we can reassure ourselves that Freud's concept of illusion is truly very far-sighted and decidedly helpful in times of crisis. Not an error, but wish-fulfilment – what more can one desire for the future of a science? And is not the ability to have illusions the only possible guarantee for the future, anyway?

It is all the more advisable, however, first of all to clarify what the full-bodied talk of psychoanalysis as the illusion of Enlightenment and disillusionment can mean. I shall try to do so by outlining quite un-systematically what traces of ideological approaches are inscribed in it and what metaphors and models of dominance are intrinsic to it. Now, these remarks may be quite trivial by professional standards, matters of course long since laid to rest, or even hair-raising verbal radicalism far departed from the practical world, unsullied by any patient and differentiating experience: all the better for the most real of realities.

2. In the beginnings of psychoanalysis, Freud the explorer (something he had been from his youth onwards and was always to remain) set out to try and investigate the depths of that 'true inner Africa', which Jean Paul, the German satirist and essayist, had already imagined to be the doubly 'monstrous' – namely huge and uncanny – realm of the uncon-scious (see Lütkehaus, 1989, 1995). And ever since then psychoanalysis has been characterised by an *explorative* and a *colonialising* impetus. For it has been typified by a will to know and an equally strong will to appropriate and dominate. Joseph Conrad's *Heart of Darkness* which was published the same year as the *Interpretation of Dreams* provides a contemporary illustration of the 'horror' which emerges when the white man colonises the heart of that double darkness.

We happily define psychoanalysis as the 'knowledge of the uncon-scious' without being aware of the enormous paradox, indeed the indelible contradiction innate in this formulation. How is it possible to have a knowledge of the unconscious? Psychoanalysis endeavours to know something about an entity which, *qua* unconscious, can at best be known by approximation and can only be approached indirectly. Indeed, seen correctly, the term should really always be placed in quotation marks. From Jean Paul via Nietzsche right through to Freud, this problematic knowledge (to the extent that it is self-reflective) remains aware of the fact that it remains the unknown variable in all human equations, the never definitively deducible 'x', as C. G. Carus has called it. Nietzsche's doctrine of the phenomenalism of the inner world turns Kant's epistemological criticism as regards the 'thing in itself' consistently inward. And what are therefore the conditions for a possible knowledge of the 'thing *in* itself', which as such is never 'for us' – neither for the patient, nor for the doctor, and certainly not a thing? Freud himself repeatedly re-affirmed Kant's epistemological reservations. Expressly citing Kant, he warned against conflating conscious perceptions of the unconscious with the unconscious processes themselves (Peter Gay, p.577). Ludwig Binswanger notes in one of his reports on his meetings with Freud (1992, p.160f.) as follows:

'Of the subjects covered in the manifold talks I was privileged to have with Freud, I would like to emphasise the following items: 1. his views on the unconscious. In the conversation in question, I had taken up a remark he had made during the Wednesday session: "The unconscious is metaphysical, we simply posit it as real!" This sentence already expresses that Freud was modest in this question. He says that we proceed as *if* the unconscious were something real, like the conscious. As a true natural scientist, Freud says nothing about the *nature* of the unconscious, precisely because we do not know anything for sure about it and instead can only deduce it from the conscious. He was of the opinion that, just as Kant postulated that behind the phenomenon lay the thing in itself, so, too, he had postulated the unconscious behind consciousness as something which, while being accessible to our experience, can itself never be the object of direct experience.'

To this extent, Pfister, who believed he could play Kant's critique off against Freud's optimism in the achievements of science (1928, p.173ff.), completely misses the mark.

It is admittedly difficult to maintain this self-critical consciousness. Thus, psychoanalysis resembles all those who claim to possess the truth (and we shall completely ignore the secessions that led into depth psychology) and whose wish for omnipotence nurtures the illusion of definitive knowledge in the form of wishes for omniscience. It accordingly pretends to know the unconscious without remaining conscious of its own constitutive limits. Not only in meta-psychology – the continuation of pre-critical metaphysics and psychology with Marx's famous 'other means' – has it often enough presented the latest news from beyond the consciousness. And it has done so as if it were at worst the cellar of our own house, in which, or so Freud's well-known theory of the three major wounds inflicted on mankind's narcissism in the course of the history of science would have it, the Ego has no longer been master ever since the psychological injury which began with Schopenhauer. The Kantian, epistemo-critical injury, and the Kantian in Schopenhauer were both factors Freud forgot, as he did Marx and the socio-economic impairment of mankind.

In Freud's thought, a knowledge of the unconscious that is certain of itself is based on a positivist understanding of science. Today, the legitimatised and therefore intensified significance of this Freudian positivism is often overlooked. Anyone who arrived on the scene with so much fantastic mental dirt surely had to offer a hard core science. However, one can side with Pfister and indeed discern other residues here: if not the claim a scientific religion lays to truth, then at least the continuation of *dogmatism as scientism*, science as the wish-fulfilling illusion of science.

The *colonialising* will to appropriate and dominate that goes hand in hand with the illusion of knowledge is even more serious. This, too, can be seen in exemplary form in the development of Freud's 'African complex' and I shall only touch briefly on it here. The correspondence with Silberstein and Ferenczi, and above all with Martha Bernays, shows clearly just how greatly the outer and inner abysses of the 'dark continent' fascinated and irritated Freud. As an explorer of the souls and a lover, what does one do in order to keep one's head above water all the same? For example, let us assume we encounter that quite *'dark continent* for psychology' – as Freud's most famous and infamous African metaphor would have it (*The Question of Lay Analysis*, p.124) – in the opaque sexual life of a small girl, and even more so in that of 'adult women'. We could presume that this allows us to hope that Freud is exercising caution and showing a certain epistemological reserve. However, this does not prevent the man, the white man Freud, from comfortingly knowing what is most important in this *dark continent* : However frighteningly potent and opaque it may be, inner Africa is swollen with penis envy!

And there is all the 'aboriginal population in the mind', 'the content of the unconscious' (1915, SE vol. XIV, p.195). It requires the missionary to colonise and domesticate it. Freud is the man who would, if only he could, prefer to baptise the instincts if this were only possible. At any rate, psychoanalysis must push ahead with damming up and reclaiming the inner swamp. Where the African or sea-like wild and stormy Id was, Ego shall be, this is the most welcome of all Freud's sentences and has meanwhile ascended to the honoured status of an object of worship, as, like no other, it fulfils the wishes of all preachers of morality and zoo directors and has never been turned around, not even in in-tellectual test runs. And the supplementary remark was added only for the record and not in some programmatic, quotable explication, namely that were Superego was, Ego shall be. What more could one want alongside a knowledge sure of itself – provided by the founder of an ecclesiomorphic organisation?

We could perhaps demonstrate this at least partial ecclesiomorphism most impressively by taking the example of one of the most revealing chapters in the history of the psychoanalytical moral science, namely its discussion of masturbation (see Lütkehaus, 1992). This enjoyable theme should not just be dealt with cursorily. I shall therefore limit myself to a few conclusions as regards the dogmatic complex and the hierarchical encrustations that correlate with it.

The original psychoanalytical scenario is, as we all know, characterised by the fact that in a magnificent act of liberation (both of himself and of others) Freud turned away from hypnotic suggestive procedures and instead opted for cathartic *chimney sweeping* by means of *free association*. This approach and the analyst's evenly suspended attention continues to be the truly explosive, anarchic element in psychoanalysis, radically different from the traditional ecclesiogenous techniques of extracting confessions: free association is shame-free and thus no confessional. Psychoanalysis has admittedly developed the habit of treating free association and interpretation exclusively as a therapeutic combination, not as two elements that exist antagonistically. And, in particular in the form of autonomous orthodox interpretative rituals, interpretation is always in danger of dwindling into self-satisfied knowledge, ascriptions (which are false attributes and prescriptions) and the corresponding wishes for empowerment. The interpreter becomes someone who intones mantras, the priest behind the couch. The illusion of a knowledge of the unconscious is the echo of an old role in which psychoanalytical enlightenment regresses to a pre-enlightenment stage. Jürgen Habermas has found such a trenchant description for this that all we need to do is change the emphasis in his expression of confidence as regards promoting communicative competence through the analytical process: 'In rulership, this process, which is geared to dissolving dependencies,' becomes inverted, 'if it [...] insists on interpretations – the addressees must have the unequivocal opportunity [...] to accept or reject the interpretations offered. Enlightenment that does not culminate in insight, i.e. in interpretations that are accepted free of coercion, is none' (1973, p.387).

That is so. It would not appear difficult to meet Habermas' conditions. But how is the interpreting analyst to avoid the suggestive power exerted by his utterly desirable knowledge? The quotation above is to be found in an essay which criticises the utopia of good rulership. With good reason: for there can be no good ruler, just as there can be no self-confident enlightener. To paraphrase Jacob Burckhardt's precise statement, power is, like definitive knowledge, not, shall we say 'actually evil', but unfailingly bad.

This leads us on to the thorny *asymmetry* of the psychoanalytical situation. In its own understanding of itself, it is intended to ensure that a situation of symmetrical communication is regained or perhaps gained for the first time (see the still highly confident portrayal by Cremerius, 1984, p.178ff.). However, both setting and procedure are diametrically opposed to such a result. And with good therapeutic cause; essay-writing dilettantes should not forget this, should they once have profited from it as patients. After all, it remains a daring undertaking to wish to create symmetrical communication at one go, indeed *on the basis* of inequality, to forge freedom through inequality and un-fraternity. Without having to draw the inverse conclusion that all asymmetrical relations are ones of hierarchical relationship, it is worth remembering now and again that hierarchical rule on principle endeavours to create asymmetry and is based on it. It has no interest at all in the destruction of illusion, in the enlightened transition into maturity. Most churches, for example, and psychoanalysis as well – to the extent that it has an institutional hierarchy – define themselves precisely as grass-roots *non*-democracies. This inevitably sounds like some late pubertal nagging wish for emancipation, after the *student revolts*. Large sections of our lives consist of situations that are asymmetrical and are for that very reason sometimes helpful. However, the implied dominance innate in asymmetry is deeply inscribed in the history of psychoanalysis and some of its basic concepts. And this was the unwelcome message behind the concept of 'mutual psychoanalysis', be it practical or not, with which the later Ferenczi revolted in an effort to recreate symmetry.

Take *transference* for example. Patients labour under it and benefit in the process of therapy from it. In the wake of the Spielrein affair, Freud and Jung shed new light on things, discovering *counter-transference* either in their own or in other *Seelenleibe* (emotive bodies). This concept itself remains entrenched in asymmetry in that from the outside it merely interprets the transference processes which unravel in the analyst as responses and thus arbitrarily and one-sidedly 'interpunctuates' communication in the analytical situation, to use Paul Watzlawick's vivid concept. That is to say, the analysts wish to uphold the asymmetry even as 'counter-transferers'. It is noteworthy to remember that from an early date Ferenczi, forever the friend of symmetry, showed a vehement interest in processes of thought transference between patient and therapist – even if this bordered on counter-enlightening spiritism. Why? Because what emerges in these processes occurs simultaneously and to an equal extent in both patient and therapist.

The concept of *resistance* also evidences similar implications as regards dominance and the illusion of enlightenment. The notion admittedly also has a good therapeutic/analytical side to it – especially when it is construed in intra-psychic terms. However, the main connotation it has, and this fits perfectly into the blind spot in the way the guild sees itself, is that of resistance as something which has to be overcome, just as defence is something to be combated. And if, as is almost unavoidable, intra-psychic resistance can only be overcome along with overcoming the inter-psychic resistance toward the analyst, then the connotation becomes problematic. For it has always been the fatherly concern of all psychologists to make certain that the poor soul does not shut itself off in defiance and obduracy. Yet the other side can certainly assume that the inclination to overcome subservience and malleability is definitely less than the propensity to overcome resistance.

I shall not bother to apply this to a psychoanalytical institutional doctrine, including a doctrine of psychoanalytical institutions. Dostoyevsky's pertinent remark that psychology is a rod with two ends could serve to promote the inevitable 'recherche de la symmétrie perdue' in psychoanalysis as well (which, however understandable and enjoyable this may be, prefers to grasp the rod at one end only). All else is illusion, wish-fulfilment, but the fulfilment of those wishes in which the holy pre-Enlightenment trinity persists, namely that trinity of self-confident knowledge, caring dominance, and asymmetry that shapes all else, protected from the illusion of Enlightenment. Nietzsche once said that 'truths are illusions, whereby we have simply forgotten that they are such.' The truth of psychoanalysis is that the illusion has been forgotten. Should we wish this illusion to have a future? Or do we even need to do so, as illusions of this type are meanwhile the only thing that still has a future?

3. The second essay written by Freud which has a title addressing the future was on *The Future Prospects of Psycho-Analytic Therapy* (1910, SE vol. XI, pp.141-151). It is well-suited as a basis for emphasising the above-outlined dogmatic/pre-critical and hierarchical elements which serve the illusion of Enlightenment and the reality of

power. At the same time, it more sharply contours the question as to the illusion of the future of the psychoanalytical illusion.

Here, Freud the sceptical realist and pessimist exhibits a truly euphoric delight in progress, for all his talk of 'depression at the magnitude of the difficulties' facing psychoanalysis. He believes there are rosy future prospects in three regards:firstly, in terms of 'internal progress', which more closely defined comprises both progress in analytical knowledge and in techniques. Freud's formulations and sentences in both areas are revealing, to put it mildly: 'We are, of course, still a long way from knowing all [that is required]' (p.141), but at least, we are well on the way to banishing 'the regularities in the structure of the different forms of neuroses [...] by means of concise formulae' and therefore shoring up 'our prognostic judgement' (p.144). The illusion of knowledge is beyond belated self-content. The 'banishing' knowledge oversteps the boundary into magic and prophecy.

From a technical point of view, things look slightly more 'friendly': the course of psychoanalytical treatment is no longer 'inexorable and exhausting' (p.141) and no longer constantly squeezes the patient. It helps the patient in identifying and overcoming his inner resistances. And the doctor has discovered 'his own complexes and inner resistances' and 'counter-transference' (p.145). However, this is interpunctuated so linearly and non-reciprocally that it first occurs 'owing to the influence of the patient on the unconscious feeling by the doctor.' It has, in turn, been possible to 'classify' the resistances. It can safely be said that we can assume that 'the most important resistances in the treatment seem to be derived from the father-complex and to express themselves in fear of the father, in defiance of the father and in disbelief of the father.' (p.144). In short, things look good for the 'increase in our therapeutic prospects' (p.147). Nevertheless, we cannot envisage 'how far the instincts which the patient is combating are to be allowed some satisfaction during the treatment' (p.145).

With this second perspective for the future, Freud quits the inter-analytical stage. The most important factors as regards the future of illusions and the future of a disillusioning science are all addressed here.

Freud predicts that the authority exercised by psychoanalysis will grow tremendously. Yet, Freud continues, the relationship between psychoanalysis and society is precarious, for the former is 'critical' of society, attributing to society a major role in causing neuroses. Psychoanalysis, Freud avers, tells society 'truths it does not wish to hear', destroys illusions, and indeed may 'endanger ideals', an accusation levelled at it. (p.147). In other words, society must be 'resisting' psycho-analysis. And this it has thus far done: The 'authority of society' and the 'force of suggestion it exerts' (p.147) are against psychoanalysis. And such authority and suggestion are anchored in 'people's inner lack of resolution and craving for authority', the strength of which 'cannot be exaggerated' (p.146). However, at the same time, reassuringly one can always count on this craving for authority, even if 'intellect' (not 'the intellectual'), is a 'power' (p.147). For this craving will in the future be to the benefit of psychoanalysis.

Freud the analyst draws (on) a striking and, as far as we can see, completely naive image to describe the change in the authority complex. For far into the Orient, 'Gentleman!', a gynaecologist is only allowed to feel the pulse on the arm which the woman stretches out to him 'through a hole in the wall' (p.147) But what avenues would not be open to him if the 'the force of social suggestion drives the sick woman' to the psycho-'gynaecologist', with whom society now conspires? He advances to the status of 'helper and saviour' of the woman – which does not prevent the theory of the analytical pulse-feeler who continues to ascribe to the imaginarily 'punctured' woman an arm erect in penis envy – one she wishes to stretch out to him but, owing to a natural defect, is unfortunately not factually able to move in this way.

As ever: even society's resistance will be overcome in the course of time and change into support – with the effect that the thrust of authority and suggestion, but not the disposition to immaturity and dominance will change.

Finally, Freud assumes the universal impact of the future hopes of psychoanalysis. In other words, the success of individual therapy will also be achieved with the mass. There will be no stopping 'psycho-analytic enlightenment' (p.150) as a whole – Freud repeatedly speaks of Enlightenment and the work of enlightenment. Fantasy worlds will be replaced by reality, mendacity by honesty, the denial of instincts by professing to have them, although this should not be confused with giving in to them.

The examples of psychoanalytically induced social progress in the guise of a process of enlightenment can thus again deliver us our *dark continent*: the peasant girls will suddenly and so thankfully cease to have hallucinations of the Virgin Mary. Or imagine an aristocratic picnic in the countryside. The ladies will no longer be able to flee into poetic paraphrasing as regards 'their natural needs'. They will have to call things by their names. Yet 'none of the men will object' (p.149), for the 'tolerance of society [...] as a result of psycho-analytic enlightenment' has made significant progress. Be it now the case of the psycho-gynaecologist, the mariologically retarded farmyards, or urinating in a field – the future has already started. Society as a whole will be transformed into 'a more realistic and creditable attitude' (p.150). And where the reality principle rules, the otherwise neurotically absorbed energy can now cry out for the overdue cultural changes: 'Allons enfants de l'Analyse / le jour de gloire est arrivé..' Great!

Well, of course it all comes with a price tag. Needless to say, now, 'thanks to the indiscreet revelations of psycho-analysis', the road to something which it is so hard to replace as the 'flight into illness' and the resulting gain in illness will be blocked. The promise of health offered is that in the future you will be able to 'face the conflict', 'fight for what you want', 'or go without it'. Nice prospects. For a few, this will hardly be an advantage. They will 'rapidly succumb or cause a mischief greater than their own neurotic illness' (p.150). For this reason, the analyst must square up to 'life not as a fanatical hygienist or thera-pist', even if on aggregate he speaks more like a psycho-Darwinist. The 'misfortune' of 'swift ruin' will 'only affect a few' and this will 'occur' swiftly. Where progress is made, a few are always left by the wayside.

Above all: even psychoanalytical Enlightenment that 'is most real-istic and creditable' will again take 'the indirect path of social authority' (p.150). The question is simply whether this has not in actual fact long since become its direct route. Overcoming resistance, and this is at any rate the core of this gay scientific message of the future opportunities of psychoanalytical therapy, terminates in authority. Freud promises that psychoanalytical Enlightenment will definitely be disillusionment, will be critique, will ensure the autonomy of a great future, while at the same time basing itself on principles which mark the limits of En-lightenment and render it illusion: namely the illusion of disillusionment.

4. But let us leave the poor, the venerable, the great Freud. Scorn and disbelief have been poured on his head for long enough. Let us instead turn to a text which most euphorically celebrates the bond between psychoanalysis and the future. I am thinking of Thomas Mann's speech on the occasion of Freud's 80th birthday (1936).

In actual fact, Thomas Mann speaks the whole time about himself, Freud, and myth, but then the future takes the place of myth – a switch in positions which makes one think twice. Mann shows himself to be truly seized by 'an anticipation of the future', a 'joyful sense of divination of the future'; indeed, the 'idea of future' is astonishingly that which he 'involuntarily likes best to associate with the name of Freud' (p.427).

In the process, Mann understands psychoanalysis less as a 'science of the unconscious' and more as a 'therapeutic method in the grand style, a method overarching the individual case' (p.427). Thanks to it, humanity will enter into a 'bolder, freer, blither' relationship to the 'powers of the underworld, the unconscious, the id.' Psychoanalytical insights change the world, because they inject a 'blithe scepticism' into things which then infiltrates the 'raw naiveté' of life, stripping it of any 'strain of ignorance' and fostering a state divested of 'patheticism'. The 'understatement' which Mann himself would know nothing of, is celebrated here as the appropriate gesture.

The twin poles Mann deploys throughout – namely 'art' or 'spirit', on the one hand, and life, on the other – are transformed here into the polarity of psychoanalysis versus life. Mann regards psychoanalysis as an ironic and yet 'artful' disillusionment of raw, unknowing life which essentially does not wish to become aware of its 'schemes and subterfuges'. And this will, Mann hopes, make it possible to heal the 'great', 'neurotic fear' and the concomitant great hatred which have hitherto governed our relationship to the unconscious powers of the underworld.

In the process, Mann provides no exact definition of how hatred goes hand in hand with fear. Is what is involved the product of a reaction, just as Thomas Mann would appear to understand hatred and fear overall as forms of reaction to the unconscious? Or does the hatred itself not give voice to the crudity and brutality of 'the powers of the lower world'? Be that as it may, psychoanalysis is up to coping with everything because it has 'worked its way through much', and knows much with its boldness, joyfulness and freedom. And it accordingly becomes 'the cornerstone for the building of a new anthropology and therewith of a new structure ... which shall be the dwelling of a wiser and freer humanity'. Its realm will be that of a 'joyfully sober world of peace' (p.428). Freud himself becomes the 'pathfinder towards a humanism of the future'. And for the 'colonising spirit and the significance of his work', his agenda for drying out the swamp of the Id is meant to foster damming and dammed Ego formation. And Freud therefore unintentionally resembles the honourable old Faust who wished to stand 'amid free folk on a free soil', the 'people of a future freed from fear and hatred, and ripe for peace'.

Quite staggering! Things have taken an hilarious turn. The most obvious explanation would be that these are words spoken at a jubilee junket. The most favourable interpretation would be that given the context of the day, the whole thing reads like one continual evocation of the 'powers of the underworld' – a panegyric attempt to discuss myth and magic. It was held in 1936 in Vienna, as if in anticipation on 8th May, three years after Hitler had been accorded power and two years prior to Austria's 'accession'. It speaks oracularly of a future humanism when the present had long since empowered barbarism. It leads to the Promised Land of freedom from fear and hatred, whilst the production of fear and hatred – and the two are not related to each other here as reactions, but are instead in keeping with a historical division of labour, carefully apportioned into race and class – is rampant. Mann sings of a peace where the Sirens of War are already shrieking. In short: he spreads the illusion of the future of joyful-human dis-illusionment. And even as regards the literary analogies of the pioneer showing the way to the Promised Land, the disillusionment has (quite illusionistically) forgotten that precisely Faust as an old man, without having had to soil his own hands, had two skeletons in the cupboard: a couple of old lovers. It is hard to find a worse omen for the future of psychoanalysis and of a humanity still to be cured of fear and hatred than this speech celebrating 'Freud and the Future'. And it is hard to imagine more drastic disillusionment.

5. The disillusionment of the illusion of the future of an illusion has meanwhile received fresh fuel which has a longer, more thorough, more comprehensive, sometimes more unobtrusive impact than a thousand-year Reich could have had. For objective reasons, the new fuel entrusts psychoanalysis far more to the past than a critique of its unprocessed and unenlightened residues could ever do.

Starting from Günther Anders' *Desideratum: A Psychology of Objects* and a discussion of Lifton & Markusen's *Psychology of Genocide* (1992), I have tried elsewhere (Lütkehaus, 1994) to show how in the age of the 'antiquated human being', as Anders termed it, (and not that secretively celebrated and declaimed by the post-structuralist or post-modern dismissal of the subject) the sciences that go hand in hand with it come up against their limits. I shall put the case with due brevity here:

According to Anders, and not just him, the world of the future will be one in which there are 'also humans', but primarily 'things', apparatuses and their dominance, that is to say 'technocracy' in the original Greek sense of the word. The concept of the totalitarianism of the commodity world (often overlooked in Anders' work) also covers this. The antiquated human being has an imagination, emotions, conscience, a complete body and soul which lag hopelessly behind compared with what he produces. The human being thus only 'co-exists in history'. 'The objects are free, the human is not.' This is the 'inversion' of history, which has become perfectly technicised and utterly commercial and which ignores the previous master of all making, indeed has dumped him in its scrap-yard precisely owing to his ruthless anthropocentrism. This adds yet another injury to the three narcissistic injuries inflicted on humanity, not to forget the Kantian and the Marxian injuries we have already appended: and this new injury takes things one step further, in that not least the humanities themselves are also affected by these injuries in the history of knowledge.

For example, human psychology, whether in the retarded form of a psychology of the individual or in the advanced form of a social psychology. How can they continue to orient themselves toward intra- or inter-subjectivity when there is neither an 'inner world' nor communication which, for all the hot air, would be worthy of the name? The communicative competence of which the out-dated pedagogues of the soul so unflaggingly speak is merely some sentimental reminiscence.

To what end all the sweet interpretative efforts, the subtle deep hermeneutics, the analytical improvement of introspection, when the one-dimensional things, be they inspired by blinkered computerised effective intelligence or by the real idiocy of the commodity world, clearly have the say, even if they have it without language or only in a programming language?

What family novels will still be written if the 'machine family' leads a harmonious life and there is no prohibition on incest to stand in the way of the endogamy of the apparatuses? King Oedipus has long since ceased to be 'the most genteel saint and martyr' in the psychological calendar; his place has been taken by the fire-bringing Prometheus with his blinding machines. Yet Prometheus has, complete with machine-based bedazzlement, long since abdicated.

Why drive ahead with a theory of instincts if the products' drive to be used and consumed (that is, beyond doubt, their death wish) long since overshadows the pitiful sexual appetites of the past? Today, the true psychology of the naked act is that of purchasing and not even the act of consumption; '*et post coitum omne animal triste*', or rather: all that then follows is rubbish.

What is the point of all the inauthentic psychoanalytical talk of 'object relations', when the objects have long since started taking over the world? Why classify fetishism as a perversion, when commodity fetishism – and it is the true fetishism — has become the norm on so vast a scale that it exceeds even the most daring dreams of past psychological or economic theorists of fetishism? That trustworthy 'Id' we so fervently remember – it is being taken literally by the machines and the commodities: it is the true subject. Ego and Superego know no ambition today other than that of becoming like the Id. And, unlike the days of Genesis, they may do so, nay, the intention is even for them to do so. Banishment from Paradise only threatens if they do not want 'to become as ...' Where Ego was, Id shall be, says the technological-commercial colonisation of the reclaimed swamp, with the human sludge deep down below. The Id is ashamed of its Ego, and the new psychology of shame knows this. And the 'goal to be learned: solidarity' – that eternal commonplace for sermons, derisible – no longer needs to be taught at all, for there is no solidarity with machines.

What about the interest in the unconscious, in that which lies beneath the surface, when there are now so many agendas that no unconscious or even 'superficiality' remains? Why still move down the dreamy '*via regia*' into the unconscious, when the expansionist dream of the machines is well on the way to becoming a reality? Control circuits, conditioning – they know and eliminate 'interruption', but the emotional meaning, the conflicts and repressions, these are a thing of the past. The new oral feedback processes are geared to principles of constancy far removed from the pleasure principle.

Why should we still want to analyse or provide therapy for processes of disassociation, when thanks to the complete liquidation of subjects not even a 'self of Auschwitz or nuclear arsenals' (as Lifton & Markusen called it) is necessary, as it was once upon a time?

Why even foster self-responsible persons, an ability to act, autonomy, when no one acts any longer, but merely 'operates' or 'serves' machines? And is conditioned by this. Why do so when triggers, whether buttons or stimuli, trigger the triggering of triggers, when objects have maxims for action and are Kantian categorical imperatives?

What is the state of psychoanalysis' sanctification of time, of slowness, when the dictatorship of speed (an essentially undemocratic principle of rotation) and what Paul Virilio has termed the 'dromocracy' that accompanies technocracy, only obey the principle of simultaneity and real time?

Why worry about the reality principle, when the brutal hard-core facts are linked up to systematic simulation on all levels?

Why still raise pathetic questions of truth? Why conduct the most absurd of all businesses doomed to failure, namely critique? Just because it is something to which we attach such importance, our once so indispensable critical critique?

In short: Why want psychological Enlightenment, when counter-Enlightenment is already the desired or already prevailing reality? Why wish to disillusion when simulations have so thoroughly undermined the devout illusions of yore that the latter are surplus to requirement? The 'gaze down the cleavage of the machines', the 'psychology of objects' — these are the now authentic finite form of positivistic, reifying 'psychologies without a soul' of yesteryear which would seem under current conditions to have more of a scientific future at any rate.

6. What has happened to a positive outlook? Have I not simply dished up utter exaggerations? Does the human being not continue to be the maker and programmer of things? Can one not continue to lie down on the couch, where the producers of such illusionary disillusionments certainly most belong? Is totalising critique, destructively bleaker forecasting not precisely the opposite of what it purports to be – namely profoundly affirmative, an echo of and applause for the purportedly attacked dominance of objects? And then there is the manifest 'pragmatic self-contradiction': Why all the effort if there is no prospect of change? Why waste time commenting on the future of psychoanalysis, if psychoanalysis has no future?

Well, psychiatry, in the form of homeopathy, includes something as hopeful as paradox intervention and intention. So let us seek solace for now in the fact that today it is not only psychoanalysis which has no future. The notion of a human future and the idea of enlightening psychoanalysis, both are the past of an illusion.

Rainer Marten

The Future of Psychoanalysis –
A Future With Whom?

Wochenpost: What does the future of music look like?
Krysztof Penderecki : If I only knew then I would start
writing exactly that way, but no one knows. All the
futurologists have conceded defeat. The best proof is
the case of communism, which no one could foresee.
I will certainly guard against even speculating.'
(January 1994)

1.   *Having a future, sharing a future*

Leading a successful life includes having a future – together with other
people, and each for himself. Future, however, such as empowers life,
is nothing outstanding or forthcoming; it is not a dimension to be
construed as empty and which is filled gradually, it is neither a reality
nor a non-reality to be explained theoretically. Humans have a future
in the practical lived present and presence of other people.

Anyone living successfully can be practically certain that they will
have a future with others and for themselves. However, practical cer-
tainties in life are not based on hard-and-fast insights. They arise only
in the course of our becoming certain of them. Succeeding as a person
in living with persons therefore means not least becoming practically
certain of the essential future for that shared life. The practice of
ascertaining this can only be shared life itself, namely the joint and
respectively individual perception of open opportunities for the practice
of life: it is in this that the ability to live rests, proves itself, gains greater
strength. Making certain of the future therefore requires jointly risking
it *together*.

In not a few cases, today anyone who is incapable of having a future with others or for himself is considered a person in need of psycho-analytical treatment. The express goal of psychoanalytical treatment is to get a patient to the point where he or she can have a future (again) and can put it at risk with others[1], or so I take the title of this volume to mean, psychoanalysis regards its own future as a problem.

Does psychoanalysis have a future? If we ask in this way, then it would appear that our own ability to live life is disturbed, if not damaged. Does the philosopher asked here suddenly find himself in the role of the person called on to administer therapy, with psychoanalysis now in the role of the person in need of the therapy? Psychoanalysis on the couch, and the philosopher behind it – what will it say, how will it start, what associations will it unleash? How will he apply his silence, his coldness in accordance with psychoanalytical technique and suspended attention, and not least his interventions? Will there be transference and counter-transference. Indeed, the question is whether psychoanalysis possesses a future. Shall we together address its 'history', that bastion of its unconscious?

No, here the problematic possession of a future is naturally not a question of how successful the therapy can be, but that of successfully sharing life. Future is not a private matter. It can only be had in a shared form. Without community and society there is no biography, no open opportunities for life.

2.   *Psychoanalysis is not avant-garde*

And this is a good thing: psychoanalysis *qua* social institution is not just a historical entity; for its own history plays a major part in defining how it sees itself. Here, the relation is like that within the Catholic Church: the Holy Book, read as seriously as it is richly quoted (as the *prima et ultima ratio*) is certainly not all it is cracked up to be. Psychoanalysis as the contemplation of humans and practical work with humans does not rest solely on Freud's writings now that it has matured into a theoretical/scientific and medical/practical institution and is in the process of developing in various other ways, too. Where it differs from the Catholic Church is in the simple fact that, while there may be various persons who would like to be its pope, there is no actual ruling pope, no institutionally anchored, inspired and thus infallible inter-pretation of the Holy Word and Will[2]. What has always counted at one time or another in psychoanalysis have been outstanding personalities with their own proposals on theory, techniques and therapy – based on their own experiences and research. The processing of these proposals has gelled into something like psychoanalysis' own history, giving it an inner unity in inexorable references back to the father. However, this unity not only does not prevent but instead actually explains that each dialogue among psychoanalysts primarily requires one thing to succeed: a culture of debate.

Anyone who positions themselves as the avant-garde does not like sharing. However, psychoanalysis is not the avant-garde, at least it is no longer. The day-dreams of a new, completely enlightened humanity which, in its pure self-illumination, is able to completely comprehend itself have, to the extent that psychoanalysis participated in them, become fully a thing of the past from any responsible point of view. 'Where Id was, there shall Ego be!' No, that can and may no longer mean for someone that in the final analysis the Ego (reason) should triumph and the Id (instincts) shall disappear and flicker out. If progress is understood as something more than just civilisational/technological advances (the practical consequence being that humans start to question their own validity), but as progress in humanity, then all that is being fostered is a bad utopia. Just as a man cannot become more masculine or a Chinese more Chinese, so humans cannot become more human – particularly as there is no human *essence*; humans are what they are *qua* the multiplicity of the human being, namely a man or woman, a child or a parent, a healthy or sick person, an employer or an employee, a Pole or a German. Whether the development of the human cortex over a few million years will turn the human into something else and what cloning the 'best' would result in – these are prospects that miss the mark by a light year when it comes to the historical human being, for whom and in whom we should seek the human being as a practical living reality.

Should some essence of the human being not be statically championed and should in particular reason brought to bear as the guideline instead then, fortunately, we cannot dream sweetly of human development henceforth being based on reason. The focus must instead be on the historical human being, as he recurs in the entire reach of the comic and the tragic as is repeatedly perpetuated, the human and the inhuman. Human history is no purposive temporal span fixated on a goal but rather is entrenched in repetition. Now, while efforts to ensure that human life and human action are practically relevant cannot be the domain of the modern avant-garde, they can likewise not fall within the ambit of post-modern theories of progress. For, among other things, these deliberately do not develop an understanding for the fact that humans endeavour theoretically and practically to shoulder the burden of psychosomatic misery – because all that counts for them is that which has a market value. In the eyes of these thinkers, anyone who does not affirm and foster some vitalist progress is a rational constructivist. In the case of Nobel Prize winner for economics, F.A. von Hayek, who has learned much from the behavioural scientists and theorists of evolution (and debates on a high intellectual level) this reads as follows:

'But the culturally most devastating effects have come from the endeavour of psychiatrists to cure people by releasing their innate instincts ... Through his profound effects on education, Sigmund Freud has probably become the greatest destroyer of culture ... We must be grateful that before this flood has finally destroyed civilization, a revulsion is taking place ... So all hope is not yet lost.'[3]

The vitalist with an evolutionist approach trammels his fear of a future for psychoanalysis by backing the opposite movement, namely vitalism. There is hardly a more trenchant way of putting the wish not to share a future with psychoanalysis. But then, with whom could psychoanalysis wish to share its 'life' in order to perhaps have a joint future and to this extent its own future?

3.   *A Future with Philosophy?*

The first disciplines that come to mind are psychiatry and internal medicine, and then the healthcare institutions and those of general social policy. It would appear self-evident that psychoanalysis cannot share life and ignore the psychosomatic (hysterical, neurotic...) misery, although precisely in this regard, as we shall try to show, sharing life is essentially problematic. What about other theorists, pioneers and practitioners working to create humane life and action? If I no longer search for the answer among others, but answer it for myself, then it is my own interest in psychoanalysis, or more precisely in the psycho-analytical situation, that makes me think of the possibility of a joint future. In the final instance, it is not the special theories that have been formed, for example libido theory in connection with dream/fear/repression/displacement and object theory as a whole that are of interest for a philosophy of successful life[4]. These theoretical attempts trace human development and human sexual (genital) self-definition, but not the encounters in which humans jointly succeed in life. It is solely the unique therapeutic situation (that pair bond of doctor and patient), based, as it is, neither on sexuality nor on a successful or fulfilling life, that, owing to what it deliberately leaves out, brings to mind successful life, a successful pair bond, both sexually and erotically speaking.

Philosophy and the psychoanalysts can have, and can dare to have a joint future on the basis of the practice and experience of the psycho-analytical situation – irrespective of the theory that informs it and poten-tially leads to a revision or further development of the theory. This demands of the philosopher that he leaves *filosofia a solo* with its solip-sistic and likewise universalistically construed rational common subject behind him and champions *filosofia in compagnia*, which derives the concepts of human individuality and human selfhood from a concept of a complex, idiosyncratically shared life. There can be no philosophical speculation on the possibilities of the continuation and change of psy-choanalytical institutions and techniques in the near and distant future, indeed of the psychoanalytical 'movement'[5]. (How will it fare in ten years time or in a century?) I shall stick with the future here in the sense of the future respectively shared and risked in the present.

4.   *The Uniqueness of the Psychoanalytical Situation*

According to Aristotle[6], humans by their nature tend to live in pairs rather than in society, and this is all the more true given that humans originally and necessarily lead communal rather than social lives. The way Aristotle sees it, humans live together not only in order to procreate but also for the sake of their own lives – so as to endure life together in community. In this view, tasks are from the outset ('immediately') shared out, and men and women have respectively different tasks. They help each other by bringing what is respectively unique to them to bear in the community. Thus, in their *philia* both the beneficial and the plea-surable are at home. They enjoy being with each other to the extent that each of them plays out his/her respective essential characteristics ($\dot{\alpha}\rho\epsilon\tau\acute{\eta}$).

I do not consider the idea outdated that a successful human rela-tionship originates in the relationship between a man and a woman as a beneficial and sensual experience. The one man with his one woman or the one woman with her one man live out a public domain which is differentiated as a domain of intimacy and of communication, whereby *communicate* means to undertake something together: they love and they need each other. However, Aristotle already overlooks the special problem of such a relationship if it is intended to endure for life. If we think it through for ourselves anew, then we soon see that such a relationship is not just based on the partners' practical certainty that they love and need each other and have a mutual past and future, but moreover rests on the practical certainty that they will at one point finally leave each other. A relationship based on love is inconceivable without a relationship based on death. And the need for each other and having-time-to-spend-together themselves already entail an awareness of the notion of death. In other words, as the psychoanalyst remarks, the idea here is not to functionalize the 'love instinct' as directed against the 'death instinct', but to see how Eros and Thanatos interact to enable human life to succeed.

However, let us address the psychoanalytical situation. A patient who decides to undergo psychoanalytical treatment in the hope that he will re-establish and enduringly strengthen his ability to lead a communal and social life (Freud speaks of the 'ability to achieve and enjoy')[7] does so because s/he suffers. Seen in terms of theoretical principles, by dint of being a son or daughter, a man or a woman, a boyfriend or girlfriend, a father or mother, or even a tenant or a subordinate he suffers from the fact that s/he cannot share authentic existence with others in a manner which is sustainable and which is life-enabling. In the process, s/he suffers fundamentally from an inability to jointly forge a successful pair-bond. A patient of psychoanalysis is, seen as an ideal type, incapable of bringing himself/herself to bear in the interaction of loving and needing each other. As an answer to this, the psychoanalyst suggests to the patient that s/he (pair) bond with him. The inability to create sustainable human relationships (the ideal type: a unique fulfilling pair bond) is thus countered with the opportunity to engage in a temporary, asymmetrical, artificial and specifically unfulfilled pair bond. In other words, in terms of form (and not of substance) a type of homeopathy is involved. Yet this form thoroughly defines the curiously allopathic nature of the psychoanalytical situation.

Not just the form, but also the substance suggest that this unfulfilled pair bond should be lent greater definition by comparing it with a fulfilled pair bond. The significant other which would seem most suitable to this end would be a fulfilled erotic pair bond. Should a pair bond (for example, between a man and a woman) reveal itself to be based on love, then part of the pair bond will entail the two assuring each other of their reciprocal love. They will, however, do this in a unique manner, namely by both putting this loving-each-other at risk.

And this is not to play Russian roulette, for both play *va banque*: in loving each other each puts his/her authentic being-as-self at stake, concentrated in the present case on the self-being-as-a-man and self-being-as-a-woman. The fundamental affective disturbance of the psychoanalytical patient, by contrast, cannot technically speaking be treated by reciprocal love and by putting this at stake. This is impossible for the simple reason that the patient is not capable of leading a communal life in the first place. There can, in other words, be no talk of him side-stepping the emotions that render him capable of life (whether himself or through reciprocity).

What, then, do the analysand and analyst constitute as a 'pair'? They do not copy or simulate a state of loving-each-other, do not find some compensation for this, and certainly do not portray a defective form of such a bond. The psychoanalytical situation is, after all, not some embarrassed predicament, not something which should not really be what it happens to be. On the contrary. It is precisely that which it is and wishes to be: an artificial situation.[8] Irrespective of how long a course of analysis lasts, in none of the repetitions does the psychoanalytical situation aspire to something in any way resembling a shared and fulfilled life as such. Rather, its unique and carefully staged characteristic is that it is not a successful life as such, but an artful and therefore artificial epoch of lively reciprocity in which the self opens up and becomes unified. What is practised in the process, initiated by the psychoanalytical technician, is not least a special type of hermeneutics.

In the psychoanalytical situation, the analyst and analysand constitute an interpretative community. Its technical-therapeutic goal is to unlock the origins of the patient's psychosomatic misery for the patient by means of relevant practical therapy. The doctor participates in the self-interpretation of the patient only to the extent that the doctor is able by means of hermeneutic interventions to help reduce resistances to the self-interpretation and thus keep in motion the psychodynamic process that the interpretation has triggered. For his part, the doctor makes new experiences which can in principle form the basis for new therapeutic insights. The asymmetry in the interpretative community thus stems not only from the fact that it is only the analysand who is being interpreted. In the ideal typical case, the analyst only participates in a technical, functional manner in the self-interpretation of the analysand. He acts quite in keeping with the Socratic 'midwife' who never intervenes with his own knowledge in the process – whereby the Other fostered by him finds his own way to wisdom. Just as no midwife can ever be the father or mother of the child in whose birth she helps, so, too, the analyst's self can never as a self be part of the psychoanalytical process which unravels 'within' the patient.

The full asymmetry of the interpretative community is thus apparent. It hinges on the being-as-self of the patient, and not that of the doctor. In terms of (self-)interpretation, the patient behaves completely artlessly, without this in any way altering the artificial nature of the situation, whereas the doctor guarantees that the situation is artificial by quite deliberately bringing himself to bear in the relationship in the role of technician. Evidently, he cannot and should not simply deny any 'personal' element. However, for the psychoanalytical situation the motto must be: as much technique as possible and as little sympathy as is necessary[9].

Even, or rather precisely when, thanks to his technically initiated and supported behaviour, the patient reveals intimate details from his life (to the other and to himself), he is incapable of being shameless in such a way that he would imbue the public character of the intimacy with a vulgar tone, strip it of any poetic basis, and indeed destroy it. Such a public status is not engendered by the artificial-technical relationship between the two. In the practical lived context of the 'hour', the patient can continue to think that it is a social public sphere which links him to the doctor. He accepts the socially-accepted method of treatment (health insurance companies), and the doctor earns his living from it. However, this life-sharing view no longer prevails in the psychoanalytical situation. The artificiality of life predominates, and with its the practical asymmetry[10].

I shall not go into the multifarious aspects of the insurmountable ambivalence of the psychoanalytical situation here, something which emerges in particular owing to the methodological reduction of a humane approach which psychoanalysis has to accomplish[11]. As such, the practical relationship between the erotic and the psychoanalytical pair bond does not call for a reduction in the elementary differences, for example it does not require a relative balance between warmth and coolness within the relationship. The therapeutic intention of using the artificial pair bond to afford the patient the opportunity to be able to enter into highly lively pair bond (again) that gives him (again) the ability to lead a life – is something which is convincing thanks not only to its homeopathic thrust, but also to its human sincerity. In the psychoanalytical situation, we see no evidence of some primordial scene of the human willingness to help. No one shares their coat with someone else, nor do they share their last scrap of bread. No blood is donated to save someone's life, and love is not kindled by love. Sharing life with someone direly in need of assistance in a gesture of voluntary help in vain – there is none of that here in the psychoanalytical situation. The psychoanalytical patient buys temporary technical assistance in life with his own money or that of a health insurance scheme. The forms of interaction in the psychoanalytical situation are not love, death and voluntary assistance in vain – but art (technique), time (*chronos*) and paying-for-something.

5. *The finiteness of analysis*

The idea of 'infinite' analysis is all the rage among psychoanalysts, precisely because there is ostensibly no end to the task of enlightenment, rendering transparent, illuminating, and fostering common sense. A new outlook is required here. For courses of analysis are in principle finite. Even analysts indicate that they accept the finiteness of analysis. This is always the case when medical practice prompts them to expose the patient no longer just to curative treatment but also to a more palliative therapy.

The driving force behind psychoanalysis, or so it should have learned from the history of its own therapeutic efforts, stems not from some animosity toward illness. Rather, its practical intention must be to enable patients to live with their suffering. It is not as if psychoanalysis approves of illness (illness as a punishment, as a lot in life, etc.). No, it remains the case that it works to bring about a successfully shared life *uti et frui* – even if psychoanalysis itself focuses not on a shared life but solely on 'achievement' and 'pleasure', by virtue of which it (intentionally or unintentionally) remains entrenched in an individualistic or solipsistic concept. There are, at any rate, psychoanalysts who do not give up if the analysand does not succeed in leapfrogging over his own difficulties – or has not yet done so, or never does. The analysand is already helped, or so runs the opinion of the person making the therapeutic effort, and even though he continues to suffer, the moment he attains a viable stance towards it, which enables him to lead a life alongside his suffering. If the analysand does not possess sufficient means of his own to afford ongoing analysis, then he remains reliant on the analyst. Such a patient is not welcome in the eyes of the state, which grants carefully controlled progress with a vitalistic thrust every possible chance, indeed is not welcome in the view of psychoanalysis as an overall institution. For, measured in free market terms, the institution is a loss-making enterprise, even when the pacifying forces which psychoanalysis exerts on behalf of state order are factored into the calculation.

Anyone who lets the ill person be ill and recognises the person who is permanently ill as a human being, is, whether he is aware of the fact or not, an opponent of any form of vitalistically-based euthanasia. Philosophers are divided on this point. Advocates of a universalistic ethics, who people the universe (in however intricately couched a way) solely with 'persons' and 'rational beings', have a simple time of it when it comes to identifying 'non-persons' and 'irrational beings', and thus casting doubts on their right to live. They are opposed, among other things, by the philosophical view that we should include in a successful shared life precisely those in need of help who are unable to create a chance for themselves of surviving in the vitalist market and keeping up with the pleasure there (whether it is dependent on persons or on reason); indeed this view suggests that the notion of a shared life centres precisely on sharing a life with these people[12]. And it is a view which is gratifyingly encouraged by the community of those psychoanalysts who believe that their medical and social action is justified not only when it is sold as a means of rehabilitation.

6.   The Finiteness of Love

The willingness to accept a 'mere' palliative essentially comprises a positive attitude towards human finiteness and thus also to the finiteness of your own efforts. Anyone caring for humans by helping them to live with their suffering is also willing to see their life and their suffering out. The lack of a will to accept death, whether someone else's or one's own, is a propensity encountered strongly among the fundamentalist believers in progress who believe that a cause is only good if it is experienced in full purity, i.e. without 'contradiction'. However, that is precisely the way life is, namely full of 'contradictions', especially if this means full of extremes and their median forms in the experience of the tolerable and the intolerable, the pleasurable and the painful, the enlivening and the sickening. One's own death, something each person's own life is fully aware of, does not lead life into a contradiction that would deny life its own essence during the course of life. Solely reason, uncoupled from serving life and given an independent form owing to worries about its universalist self-survival, adopts a vantage point from which its champions insist life must remain life 'without contradiction'

– the position is deeply otherworldly, and is indeed inimical to life. Psychoanalysis, with its enlightening thrust, is also predestined to miss the practical meaning for life of death. In practice, the meaning it associates with human suffering can hardly be coupled with a meaning for dying and death. The notion of self-relationship I use in what follows is intended to clarify why finding a meaning for death actually focuses on the practice of life.

A patient who expressly and symptomatically conveys to an analyst that he feels compelled to commit suicide – has no death of his own. If the expression 'my own death' is used then it highlights a successful self-relationship, as can be the case with the expression 'my own life', 'my own gender', 'my own feeling', 'my own age'. If we think about human relationships which succeed, then the notion of self-reference must be included in our thoughts.

My life, my *own* life – in the case of a person successfully sharing life, of a relationship imbued with self, which is understood by the Other and understands the Other – construes the self both *within* and as the relationship. The Other, without which there can be no self-rela-tionship to 'own' and to 'my', is present in its relation to self. A practical self-reference never exists other than in the unity of the reciprocal presentation of self in the face of both the Other and one's self.

Self-relationships are never to be interpreted in terms of singularity or solitude. They quite fundamentally entail relationships in which life is shared. The human being-as-self should not be interpreted onto-logically or in terms of a metaphysical philosophy of the individual, but practically. It simply indicates the practical positioning of the one and the other in self-related and unique togetherness. Your own life includes leading a life together with others and with yourself. The same is true of everything you live *practically* as your own. In the process, the self-relationships do not entail some simple random addition. For example, your own death forms a constitutive part of your own life and *vice versa*. Thus, the answer to the question of whether psychoanalysis has a future, if provided from the vantage point of a successful life, depends on what psychoanalysis considers to be our respectively 'own' life and death (as a unity). The philosophical insight that an affirmative relation to life must include an affirmative relation to death (and *vice versa*) has to do with love.

What we see most clearly in the erotic and in the most excitingly tense, practical lived relationships, in which the forces of gender recipro-cally demand those of the other as the most attractive and enlivening forces possible, is the unique human form of sharing life. In love, it is the act of animating which *itself* unites the one with the Other. For this reason, the most exciting encounter of forces in a shared life, should the loving-enlivening aspect succeed, is also in itself the most successful balance of forces. And just as it is the most enlivening aspect, so, too, it is the most finite. For, whether the one or the Other is aware of the fact or not, or wishes to be aware of the fact or not (indeed, irrespective of what the facts of the matter may be), as an act the loving-enlivening aspect is geared to death and thus touches on something which gives life its final stability and keeps it in check.

In the context of love, we should not always ask whether it is of such a quality that it can endure and provide resilience and whether in fact it would not be more appropriate to get used to the fact that it does not. Instead, it would be better to simply consider that love uniquely clears a path for humans, enabling them to give their life stability. For it is love which convey deaths to people in a way that could quite simply *not* be more significant for us. The issue here is the death of the beloved and your own death, which, thanks to the reciprocal nature of the loving relationship, is also the death of the beloved. 'My beloved' uttered by both is a phrase which, in order to apply unconditionally, must be said until death, until the death of the one and of the Other. Conversely, we cannot speak of death if it does not have such supporting significance for practical life in the form of the two lover's wish for love 'till death do us part'. Love could not make life so precious without death, nor could death make life so precious without love.

7.   *The Id and the Ego – philosophically speaking*

Allow me now to interpret what I have said differently and to speak ostensibly of something completely different, namely the Id and the Ego. The own Ego, the own Id – what is the state of affairs as regards the self-reference of Id and Ego? Let us take the Ego, without troubling ourselves too much about the definition, as the agency of interpretation and justification imbued with self. Then, the Id can be considered the agency imbued with self that is interpreted and justified, but it is also that which is never completely exhausted by the definitions and justifications given by the Ego. To this extent, the Id is likewise also the agency of that which can in the final instance not be interpreted or justified. This is precisely the reason why not everything can become Ego. That part of the Id which has been interpreted and already justified (tamed) is, after all, already Ego. In the final analysis, the Ego, in order not to be all of 'reality' and thereupon to implode, needs there to be a residue in the Id which cannot be interpreted or justified – quite simply because it requires the Id.

The reference of Id and Ego as imbued with self succeeds as life if it is balanced, relatively speaking: the Ego's ordering power ($\kappa\rho\acute{a}\tau o\varsigma$) does not overwhelm the Id, and the Id's untamed power ($\beta\acute{\iota}\alpha$) does not overwhelm the Ego. The Id is just as much a necessary part as is the Ego as regards enabling life as a shared life that is grounded, tested and strengthened. We would therefore do well to reform the programmatically abused claim 'Where Id was, there shall Ego be!', to read:

Where Id is, there shall Ego also be, and shall exert its not over-powering power!

Where Ego is, there shall Id also be, and shall exert its not over-powering power!

When its power is balanced thanks to the Id, the Ego stands for the enlivening liveliness and enlivening deadliness of life. The balance such as is struck by the successful relationship of Ego to Id as imbued with self entails the Ego being enlivened and also being given a clear end. In other words, the Id is by no means external to the Ego. Rather, it works through the relationship to the Ego within itself. In this manner, the Id no longer construes itself as the inimical and repelling opposite, but instead discovers itself as the unique intimate companion of the Ego: it is closer to the Ego than the latter is to itself, for all its possible self-transparency. The Ego is therefore no longer understood as some free-floating practical position. To the extent that an able and life-enabling life is led, the Ego is that practical position of the enlivening liveliness and deadliness of life. Id and Ego are not two entities, but they also do not coincide. They are the necessary two Ideas innate in the one Idea of life. Your own Ego, your own Id – this is one and the same relationship to self. I believe we can use the following formula to denote how to strike a balance between the powers, and this is required for a successful relationship to self: As much Id as possible, as much Ego as necessary.

Your own Ego, your own Id – as such, everything which is your own requires the other. If a person's own relationship between Id and Ego is disturbed, then it requires the artificial other – psychoanalysis as a therapeutic institution. Let us assume, however, that the theoretical constructs of Ego and Id do not remain reserved for pathological cases, as Freud wished, and that we instead use them fruitfully for the philosophy of a life that succeeds – as the basis of successfully sharing life. Then they will first truly discover that they are 'own' or 'mine' only on the basis of practical relationships in life. Be that as it may, the interhuman dimension is the original location of Id and Ego – and not the intrahuman level. Relationships to self are from the outset and in the end relationships of shared life. In sharing life, all this is risked primarily in the successfully achieved self-relationship of Ego and Id: your own life, your own love, your own death.

In the flux of presenting considerations on human life this side of utopia and acceptance in the form of hypotheses, we may have lost sight somewhat of the future of psychoanalysis. However, appearances are misleading, as these considerations finally comprise the widest-ranging assumption possible, namely that philosophy itself has an interest in the future of psychoanalysis.

NOTES

[1] Wolfgang Loch, *Perspektiven der Psychoanalyse*, (Stuttgart, 1985).

[2] The fictitious possibility of absolute Freudian orthodoxy is precisely that: fictitious. For a corresponding discussion of the problematic quality of scientific objectivity in psychoanalysis under the precondition that the assessors are homogenous (e.g. that they have all appropriated Freud in exactly the same way), that there is a consensus among experts, that the consensus is shored up empirically, and that the clinical constructs have exactly the same meaning (the coincidence of observation and interpretation), see H. Thomä et al, 'Das Konsensusproblem in der Psychoanalyse,' in: *Psyche*, 11(1976), pp. 979-1004.

[3] F.A. von Hayek *Three Sources of Human Values*, (LSE, 1978, pp. 28, 29, 30).

[4] see my *Lebenskunst*, (Munich, 1993).

[5] For a diagnosis of its present decline as regards research methodology, claims to scientific status, and the institution of training analysts and training analysis, see J. Cremerius, 'Spuren-sicherung. Die "Psychoanalytische Bewegung" und das Elend der psychoanalytischen Institution,' in: *Psyche*, 40 (1986), pp.1068-89.

[6] *Nicomachean Ethics*, VIII, 14, 1162a 17ff.

[7] See C. Nedelmann, 'Nach Möglichkeit leistungs- und genußfähig machen. Betrachtungen zum psychoanalytischen Behandlungsziel,' in: *Jahrbuch der Psychoanalyse*, 30 (1993), p. 101

[8] Loch states in his *Zur Theorie, Technik und Therapie der Psychoanalyse* (Frankfurt/Main, 1972, p. 183) that the partner relationship in psychoanalytical treatment unravels 'not at the real level but in the form of an 'as-if' relationship'. This is an inaccurate description of the position of both the doctor and the patient. The relationship as a whole consists of an artificial-technical reality, yet at the time this reality leaves nothing to be desired. This excludes from the outset any reasoning 'as-if' in the Kantian sense. An 'as if the patient loved him' is just

as inconceivable as is an 'as if he were his patient'. And the patient, too, does not know how to stage an 'as-if' setting as regards the doctor, that is unless he bids farewell to the psychoanalytical process

[9] For emphatic affirmation of the role of technique and the associated coolness in the psychoanalytical situation see, for example, Leo Stone, *The Psychoanalytical Situation* (1961); for the opposite attempt to inject as much warmth as possible into the situation see, for example, A. J. W. Holstijn, 'Über das Schweigen des Patienten und das Liegen bei der psychoanalytischen Behandlung,' (1961) in: L. Salzmann et al (eds.), *Fortschritte der Psychoanalyse. Internationales Jahrbuch zur Weiterentwicklung der Psychoanalyse*, vol. 1, (Göttingen, 1964).

[10] This is not only not contradicted by the fact that the two understand themselves as partners in the way they construct their special relationship. Indeed, precisely such an understanding is called for. Without partnership, it would not only not be possible to tolerate the artificiality and practical asymmetry, these would not even arise in the first place. Cremerius consequently speaks of 'partner-like dealings' (in his 'Die Konstruktion der biographischen Wirklichkeit im analytischen Prozeß,' in his *Vom Handwerk des Psychoanalytikers. Das Werkzeug der psychoanalytischen Technik*, vol. 2, [Stuttgart & Bad Cannstatt, 1984], p.400) and Loch (*ibid.*) talks of a 'relationship of partners'.

[11] For a comprehensive portrayal of this ambivalence, see my 'Die psychoanalytische Situation und der Augen-Blick,' in S. O. Hoffmann, *Deutung und Beziehung. Kritische Beiträge zur Behandlungskonzeption und Technik in der Psychoanalyse*, (Frankfurt/Main, 1983), pp.49-65.

[12] This is not meant in the sense of the communitarians, because the view does not hinge on prescribing some norms or others for humans (e.g. equality of the sexes' or 'social justice'). A conscience that wishes to inform shared life is generated precisely by sharing such a life.

Jürgen Körner

The Professionalisation of the Profession of Psychoanalyst

1. Introduction

It would seem that it ought to prove possible to bring the profession-alisation of the profession of psychoanalyst to a preliminary end in the near future. New legal conditions governing the profession and new social legislation have secured the provisional structure under which physicians and graduate psychologists learned the profession of psy-choanalyst and practised it. The newly created title of specialist doctor in psychotherapy offers physicians certain access to a professional career. And the German Law on Psychotherapists will liberate psy-chologists from depending on patients being 'officially transferred on to them' by doctors, a situation often felt to be degrading. Further training institutions recognised and supervised by the state will replace the old, privately managed psychoanalytical training institutes. Persons who complete such further training, whether originally doctors or graduate psychologists, can be sure that they will permanently be able to claim payment of their fees from the health insurances companies. These changes clearly reveal that psychoanalysis has gained and shored up much public recognition as a therapeutic method.

State supervision and legally reinforced claims to a monopoly on a service are the pinnacle of a process of professionalisation that com-menced some 85 years ago. In 1910, psychoanalysts set up the first courses of study; since that time, access to the profession has been the product of further training. The curricula became increasingly differ-entiated, while offices and hierarchies became established, and standards today govern entrance to further training courses and diplomas, while scholarly exchanges and publications are characterised by a focus on quality.

The growing public recognition has paid off: in 1967 in Germany psychoanalytical / therapeutic services were made part of the range of treatment covered by health insurance schemes. By contrast, it appeared fairly piffling that psychoanalysts gradually lost any specialist responsibility for the further training, that 'the presence of a third party [the specialist providing the expert opinion] was now defined within the system' (Cremerius, 1992, p.70) and that access to further training became the exclusive preserve of doctors and psychologists. All the others, all the theologians and sociologists, pedagogues and historians have since been prevented from receiving professional training to become psychoanalysts.

These are indeed severe disadvantages. By limiting the professions which may have access to further training to those of medical practitioners and psychologists, the scientific and methodological spectrum of psychoanalysis has been narrowed, and, moreover, growing state control of curricula and final examinations subjects psychoanalytical postgraduate training to outside influences. The disappearance of the professional title 'psychoanalyst' into the much broader term 'doctor for psychotherapeutic medicine' or 'psychological psychotherapist' serves to dismantle the uniform professional psychoanalytical identity; furthermore, the classification of psychoanalytical / therapeutic services under healthcare cost plans compels psychoanalysis to compete on unfair terms with medical services. It threatens the income of psychoanalysts and prevents patients from having ready access to psychoanalytical treatment.

Has it nevertheless been worthwhile ensuring state recognition? Are the costs of professionalisation low enough to justify the results? And: how will psychoanalysis go forward further now that professionalisation has advanced so far here?

2.   *Professionalisation of the profession of psychoanalyst*

Professionalisation generally serves to transform an occupation into a profession and a source of income (Titze, 1989). The first precondition for this is that professional activity must be distinguished from lay treatment. For example, everyone should realise that a psychotherapeutic dialogue differs from a discussion with helpful friends. In such a case, the actions of a professional must be learned and courses of study established which culminate in a diploma according to a pre-defined standard. Professional associations are regularly formed which offer such courses, define the goals and supervise the results. Sooner or later, such training courses will also function as the eye of the needle and will, therefore, not infrequently serve as a means of artificially limiting numbers.

Successful professionalisation leads to the social recognition of a profession, above all if the specific professional representative body conducts scholarly research and efficiently monitors adherence to professional norms. In the ideal case, state recognition of a profession leads to those accorded such recognition likewise holding a monopoly on their services and all other persons being prohibited from offering the like. And if the profession thus developed is valuable or even necessary for a society, then members of the profession can expect that their services will also be paid for from public coffers, or the fees at least fixed for the profession as a whole.

The profession of medical doctor is an example of successful professionalisation. In point of fact, the activity of a doctor can almost always be distinguished clearly from the assistance of a lay person. A rigidly organised and watchful professional representative body (and all doctors are compelled to be members of this 'club') ensures adherence 'within' the profession to the due professional norms and on the 'outside', and creates effective political and material clout, while also helping to shape the design of training and further training.

By contrast, the example of the profession of teacher, in particular those working with the handicapped or disadvantaged, is often considered only 'semi-professional' (Dewe & Otto, 1987), as the activity of a teacher cannot always be clearly distinguished from the actions of a well-meaning person and because there has been no success in turning this profession into a sure source of income. The public respect accorded teachers also leaves much to be desired (in Germany), and establishing the corresponding courses of study has certainly not led to a sufficient range of commensurately remunerated jobs being established.

Any process of professionalisation entails an increase in bureaucracy (Terhart, 1990). Offices and a corresponding hierarchical structure come into being, forming a ladder for professionals to climb in the course of their careers. Tasks are increasingly divided up, individuals are sworn into their positions and are expected to act loyally toward the organisation or institution of which they are members. As a consequence, the scope for individual action becomes less for all involved, and decisions are no longer made to 'the best of an individual's knowledge' and with a clear conscience, but according to what is expected of the person holding office.

The qualifications of someone holding office are judged in terms of whether they fulfil the expectations associated with his office – not with his person. It is not informal criteria that should decide on the career of someone in office, and not how well liked he is or his appeal as a person, but the openly discussed quality with which he invests his office. This, after all, is a desirable side to the emergence of a bureaucracy, for it reduces the informal spread of power and influence in favour of public control. Given that individuals can now plan their professional advancement or career, they also place themselves at the service of the organisation which offers them a hierarchy of offices and tasks.

For many years now, psychoanalytic institutions, expert associations, and institutions of further training have undergone a process of bureaucratisation. Steep hierarchies have arisen. A colleague starts out as an applicant for further training, attends lectures, becomes an examinee, then a trainee, and, after his or her exams, an institute guest, perhaps a permanent guest, or may go on to become a member of the institute or of a local working party, perhaps even a lecturer, and is subsequently commissioned to handle training analysis and supervision analysis, finally perhaps becoming a training analyst, chairing some further training committee, replacing a retiring member on a board, etc.

Alongside this gradual emergence of a bureaucracy, psychoanalytical institutions have nevertheless upheld certain familial structures that run counter to bureaucracy. For all the formal hierarchies, smaller institutions of further training, in particular, are run by groups which usually consider themselves a group of friends or at least a group of like-minded professionals. Usually, they have no statutes stipulating the duties of each individual in his particular office. The majority of the decisions, the appointment of new members, the nomination of lecturers, and commissioning of training analyses may all involve formal votes being taken, but are in fact based on decisions taken on the basis of informal agreement. There are no controversial discussions, and certainly no rational, readily tangible justifications for or against a particular decision.

The *status of training analyst* is an especially striking example of the curious mixture of bureaucratism and family basis in psychoanalytical institutions. The training analyst holds an office which accords him great respect both within the institution and beyond. Only he is permitted to offer personal analysis to participants in further training and as a rule he alone is responsible for carrying out supervision. Now, while training analysts form their own body within all institutes, as members of this body they do not have a discernible task, just as they do not as individuals have specific duties; the only task of the body would appear to be to appoint new training analysts, in other words to suggest who should be the next generation.

The exceptionally high social status of training analysts and their influential work contrasts starkly with the mechanisms which regulate their appointment. All institutes of further training, as well as the expert associations and the psychoanalytical umbrella association (e.g. in Germany the DGPT) award the title 'training analyst', but they do not use any criteria in their selection procedures that do real justice to the matter at hand. The only criterion subject to public control is the simple requirement that a person must have spent some years as a colleague engaged in further training at the local institute. All other criteria are a matter of informal agreement. I am thinking of scholarly reputation, personal standing among colleagues, loyalty to one's own institute, etc.

It would seem that the status of a training analyst indicates that the professionalisation of the psychoanalytical profession has not been entirely successful. For the division of tasks may well have spawned specific offices (such as that of training analyst), but it has failed to subject access to this office and holding it to public control.

Further psychoanalytic training itself somehow seems not quite to fit the state of professionalisation of the psychoanalytic profession – both in terms of *content* and of *methods*. On the one hand, over the last 25 years institutions of advanced psychoanalytical training have taken on board countless features exhibited by state-controlled curricula, partly voluntarily and partly in response to the material blessing of psycho-therapeutic services now being included in the health insurance remuneration schemes. They have formalised the curricula with the assistance of study rules and examination statutes that withstand even litigation. They have founded curricula on which teaching is based and given it a didactic foundation (planning of graduate courses structured as a series of semesters, deliberations on the relation between teaching contents and how they can be imparted in class). They have improved the teaching methods by incorporating different media, transcripts of therapy sessions and even by using video recordings of initial interviews. The students progress from one stage of qualification to the next, are assessed frequently, and have to present an extensive project, including a case study; in some institutes they are also required to have published before being eligible for graduation.

On the other hand, giving psychoanalytical further training clear scholarly roots is a project that would seem to have failed. All the teachers in the further training institutions are themselves psychoanalysts, but hardly any of them is specifically qualified to teach psychoanalysis. Neither do such teachers have a proven track record of teaching or didactic expertise (is every good psychoanalyst also a good teacher of psychoanalysis?) nor have they all learned to reflect in scholarly terms on psychoanalytical theory. They take little account of the findings of research in related scientific disciplines (e.g. cognitive psychology, developmental psychology, neurobiology) and seldom take part in philosophical discussions or specifically those on scientific theory. What they offer is psychoanalysis the way they personally see it – and it is this which they reveal in their seminars on psychoanalytical text and in their casuistic contributions.

Given the state of affairs in further training one would wish that professionalisation must lead swiftly to public control of all posts, especially that of training analyst, improve the quality of teaching during further training, and ensure that teaching staff have the requisite scholarly and pedagogic qualifications. However, before that happens (and I have no doubt that it will happen), some arguments need to be discussed which cast a different light on the state professionalisation has reached to date.

An example here would be the professionalisation of the profession of teacher. Until the 1960s, teacher training in Germany was left in the hands of the old 'Pedagogic Colleges' (teacher training colleges). The teachers there were primarily teachers, not specialist scholars. The students learnt the way their teachers understood their pedagogic tasks, but they still learned little about the didactics of the subjects they were later meant to teach. Such training was soon suspected of having too thin a scholarly base and the colleges were dissolved and their activities integrated into university teacher training programmes.

The teachers trained at German universities today acquire strong specialist didactic skills in subjects such as mathematics, foreign languages, or geography. But they have difficulties acquiring the relevant pedagogic skills. Their first encounter with pupils often leaves them feeling unable to cope. The 'shock of the real' is a symptom of an unsuccessful transition from university to the world of schools. The reason for this crisis is often to be found in the fact that teacher training students often have little contact with teachers during their training, but learn a lot from psychologists, sociologists, philosophers, and, above all, specialists.

Graduates of standardised scientific courses are therefore trained as 'experts' (Terhart, 1990, p.151) and possess highly specialised practical skills – but they do not have the specific attitude necessary for the job, namely the professional ethic, something which evidently cannot simply be assembled from the bits of specialist scholarly training they receive. To this extent, the professionalisation of teacher training has failed, primarily because there has been a one-sided emphasis on scientific standardisation (Schwendenwein, 1990).

Could it not be that psychoanalytical training faces a similar dilemma: that the professionalisation of further training could indeed raise the level of teaching courses though it would fail to impart a professional ethic for psychoanalysts? And that the practice of training to date may not meet didactic and specialist standards but is indeed suited to inculcating the professional ethic of the psychoanalysts, because the student is confronted by a teacher whose attitude and stance towards the theme, towards the subject matter embodies the professional ethic of the psychoanalyst?

3.   The professional ethic of the psychoanalyst

The development of a professional ethic is the best yardstick for the progress of professionalisation (Terhart, 1990). Successful professionalisation protects the professional ethic and allows it the space to flourish. Now what is the professional psychoanalytical ethic and to what extent does the professionalisation of the psychoanalytic profession promote it?

The professional psychoanalytical ethic prescribes what rules shall govern the actions of a psychoanalyst in the course of his work, what he should and should not do in certain situations. Generally speaking, to follow the model Niemeyer (1990, p.85) gives for the professional pedagogical ethic, we could say that the professional psychoanalytical ethic rests on ethical and professional autonomy, on relative autonomy *vis-à-vis* institutional ties, and on responsibility toward the patient. This very general definition of ethical and professional autonomy needs to be given greater precision. What I have in mind is a group of *attitudes* (an exemplary model is Mertens on the abstinence rule, 1992, p.1) which together form a *stance* (e.g. Kutter *et al*, 1988), but what I am also thinking of is *knowledge for action* and '*knowledge for change*' (Thomä & Kächele, 1985), supported by the reflected use of the psychoanalytic method (e.g. Faimberg, 1987; Körner, 1990).

In the case of the professional psychoanalytical ethic it is obvious that there is apparently no binding *canon of regulated knowledge*; the 'technical' concepts such as 'abstinence', 'free association' and 'suspended attention' quite clearly do not specify what the psychoanalyst should do in the treatment situation. In fact almost the opposite is true. Some concepts have a negative thrust, such as abstinence, while others are geared to a utopia, such as those of suspended attention and free association. Yet again, there are others such as that of 'working alliance' (Deserno, 1990), 'therapeutic Ego splitting' (Körner, 1989) and 'real relationship' (Ermann, 1992) which, while not specifying the rules for therapeutic procedure nevertheless do impart a conception of what a positive psychoanalytical / therapeutic relationship can be.

The *psychoanalyst's stance* stems less from his obedience to a group of rules for action and more from his conception of the *psychoanalytic relationship*. This could be characterised as follows. The analysand suffers from inner conflicts and seeks help in order to find more satisfying and less painful solutions for them (A.-M. Sandler, 1988, p.3). We, the psychoanalysts, offer him a therapeutic relationship in which he can unfold his conflicts in the form of unconscious relation phantasies. We allow him to unravel his inner conflicts as conflicts of relationship within the 'framework' of the psychoanalytic situation (Bleger, 1968) by using us (Sandler, 1976) as objects of projected identification.

The analyst's contribution here initially consists of the willingness to permit the analysand to make use of the object – it is, as it were, a transitional relationship. As analysts, we expose ourselves to the transference phantasies, allow ourselves to be addressed as the threatening mother, the seductive father, or the envious sibling, and we experience all these possibilities. We concede that we are envious or seductive or threatening, we feel what that would really be like, but we do not act that way.

The transference relationship is a highly serious relationship for both sides, involving sincere feelings[1]. We enable the unconscious transference phantasy to emerge discernibly in the reality of the analyst/ analysand relationship by 'fictionalising' (Raguse, 1992) our conversation with the analysand; we treat it as a literary text or as a dream which points to something concealed, a latent meaning.

Healing in the psychoanalytical process is something we achieve by interpreting on behalf of the analysand the impact of his transference phantasy in the concrete situation and, while interpreting, also indicating that we accept our part in the conflict-laden dyad – in other words, as analysts we do not deny the part we play or try and turn it on its head. By talking in this way about the relationship we offer the analysand an 'eccentric vantage point' (Körner, 1990a) from which he can view us and himself from the outside. This enables him to leave the transitional relationship behind him and thus stop using the analyst as an object who does not exist 'for himself' but 'for the analysand'.

Needless to say, we do not bring about change simply by acquainting the analysand with the error of his transference, with his reminiscence of old relational phantasies. Such indications and reconstructive interpretations serve as visualisation rather than to effect change. As a rule, change means the integration of parts of the self which could not hitherto be integrated (Daser, 1991). This presupposes a 'prior achievement' (Ermann) by the analyst, namely that he has worked through the relational phantasy offered him.

The precondition we analysts must fulfil as persons – the core of our professional stance – entails our being able to accept the projected transference phantasies (Loch called it 'tasting' the transference) and identify with them, but limiting this identification and being able to 'let go' of it again. This presumes a relative independence from our own inner objects, a not overly great fear of our own unconscious, and elastic powers of resistance.

In such a concept there is no space for giving the goals of analysis an operationalised form. There is also no point of reference from which the analysand's transference could be 'measured'. The meaning of the procedure is, after all, to move the analysis forward – not towards a goal, but by *deconstructing* the existing reality of relationships, rendering the present compromises and attempted solutions (such as, for example, projective identification) visible and shedding light on the unconscious background to them. In this context, we analysts must also be expected to fictionalise our own understanding of ourselves and the solutions to conflicts in our own biographies. Otherwise, we would not be able to allow the relationship offered (it is one that often bears very 'evil' traits) to take life within us.

This conception of the psychoanalytical relationship explains why the concepts of the psychoanalytical relationship are so useless as rules in the sense of a goal-oriented knowledge of change. The rule of abstinence, the doctrine of the working alliance and of a real relationship, and in particular the commitment to uphold free association all serve to deconstruct the conceptions of the analysand and of the analyst as regards their current reality, their goals, and their intentions. And it enables the two to experience the obscured origins of these in unconscious phantasies. These 'rules' actually create a frame for a situation, the reality of which thus becomes a fiction and in which the unconscious intentional thrust that is concealed behind conscious intentions then becomes visible.

Even if the psychoanalytical process runs an 'aimless' course in this respect, there is nevertheless an intention behind it. In the final analysis it is intended to help the analysand find an acceptable and less painful solution for his inner conflicts (A.-M. Sandler 1988, p.3). However, neither the analysand nor the analyst can anticipate this solution; it is not present like a goal that they can aim for. Instead the two jointly develop the reality for a relationship as a new construct in which they both have a changed place.

Psychoanalytical work consists of oscillating between 'surrendering' to the unconscious and comprehending, of considering things from an 'eccentric' vantage point. One of these poles alone would not suffice: by devoting themselves solely to the unconscious phantasy, the analyst and analysand would lose themselves in a utopian space in which everything would be possible but everything would be the same. And simply by grasping things the patient might adjust perfectly to given social circumstances, but would not succeed in creating a new reality for relationships.

Freud's 'technical' concepts exhibit this *dual character of dedication and control* . His concept of transference ('false connection', Freud & Breuer, *Studies in Hysteria*), for example, enables the analyst to surrender himself to the patient's unconscious transference phantasy owing to the serious, 'genuineness of the love' (Freud 1915a, SE vol. XII, p. 168) while retaining 'control' of this phantasy by dint of viewing it with distance, through reconstruction and interpretation.

4.   *Professional ethic and professionalisation*

The professional psychoanalytical ethic interacts fruitfully with the professionalisation of the profession of psychoanalyst. On the one hand, the process of professionalisation affects the professional psychoanalytical ethic and should serve to preserve it and move it forwards. On the other, psychoanalysts thus give professionalisation a direction which accords with their conception of the professional ethic.

The advantages of professionalisation are obvious: it offers an increasing ability to withstand the challenge of the scholarly competition and it is the enticing prospect of being successful in the domain of health policy with objective data on successful therapies at a time when economic competition is becoming more fierce and public coffers more empty. The uncertainty of participants in further training about their own progress and their fear of exams could thus at long last be brought to an end. Whereas they had hitherto feared that it was their loyalty to their local institution or the suitability of their character that was being tested (more or less covertly), they can now hope that examinations and colloquiums will concentrate on qualifications that can indeed be tested, namely knowledge and measurable competence in therapy.

If we consider the impact of professionalisation on the professional psychoanalytical ethic then it is very easy to be highly critical. The propensity among psychoanalysts when squaring up to competing therapeutic methods (and in light of sharp criticism about how serious their own theory is) is to objectify therapeutic goals and to present the paths taken by psychoanalytical therapy as being intersubjectively valid, which undermines their ability to look beyond the immediate relationship and perceive the unconscious phantasy beyond the reality. The more they succeed in abstracting from the subjectivity of their personal impressions when describing psychoanalytical processes, and the more it becomes possible to give the goal of therapy an operational form, the stronger the control element in their cognitive method becomes, but the element of submission is lost. Their descriptions become more unambiguous and more comparable, but they shed their metaphorical ambivalence, their wealth of associations and their character of allusion atrophies.

The state of affairs as regards psychoanalytical further training is analogous. Overly scientific contents and graduate courses shackled to curricula may clarify what the 'object' of the psychoanalytical method is, and permit all the teachers and students to be able to gauge the success in learning[2]. However, here again there is a disadvantage, for the candidate learns the concepts and learns how to apply the methods, but the professional ethical stance of the psychoanalyst, the intermediary position between surrender and control, remains alien to him.

If psychoanalysts today bemoan the consequences of the professionalisation of their profession and in particular the fact that the profession's structures have become institutional and bureaucratic, then this most probably stems from the fact that they feel the full brunt of the disadvantages.

Without a doubt, psychoanalysts find themselves confronted by an almost intractable dilemma. On the one hand, there are many respects in which the professionalisation of the psychoanalytic profession has been successful. It has led to social recognition; moreover, psychoanalytic activity presumes a regulated training, and those who complete it offer their services as a monopoly and according to a fixed scale of fees. On the other, the (unavoidable?) institutionalisation of psychoanalytical training increasingly comes into conflict with the professional psychoanalytical ethic, as the psychoanalyst's work is geared to perceiving the unconscious phantasies in the fictitious reality of the transference relationship. Psychoanalysts as members of a professional grouping are forced to found their identity formation on defence mechanisms with which they create unconscious properties that have a dynamic impact, as Beland (1983) writes. As individuals, they face an almost impossible task: as training analysts conducting training analysis, for example, they must see through those defence mechanisms on which their own status is based and, as lecturers, must use concepts, whose ambiguity and associative reach are truncated by institutional defence mechanisms. And as members of a professional group they create the bureaucratic structures whose stability is due to their meaningfulness being accepted by all those involved. However, psychoanalytical work is geared to the perception of the non-rational unconscious phantasy precisely within what is rationally and mutually accepted.

This dilemma, and it is one psychoanalysts inevitably face, shapes not only their professional ethic, but also their institutional and bureaucratic structures. This enables us, for example, to gain a better understanding of the strangely contradictory conditions underlying the *organisation of further training*. For all their questionable pedagogic and expert abilities, ostensibly out of date and unprofessional lecturers guarantee that the professional psychoanalytical ethic is imparted to students – if only because they present their 'objects of study' in their capacity as psychoanalysts and therefore convey a feeling for their psychoanalytical stance. In other words, if a psychoanalyst lectures on defence mechanisms he does so perhaps in a less differentiated and precise manner than would a cognitive psychologist, for example. However, he indirectly also talks about how he himself takes up the analysand's resistance and sees in it the unconscious phantasy the analysand seeks to defend against. In the language of psychoanalytical lecturers, the concept of defence (like the other clinical and methodological concepts) thus retains its 'floating' quality, its contradictory form half-way between submission and control.

On the other hand, the psychoanalyst who brings his psychoanalytical stance to bear in a modern, professionalised institute of further training seems strangely antiquated. He will be suspected of painting a mystified picture of the psychoanalytical method as a stance of pure *submission* to the unconscious and of ensuring that the theory of treatment techniques cannot be subjected to rational control. In particular, the narration of case studies so typical of the teaching methods used by psychoanalysts has come in for criticism (e.g. Spence, 1989; Meyer, 1994), as it is notoriously 'obliging' to the narrator and his concepts and does not permit alternative conclusions. The language of casuistry is metaphorical and full of allusions, the claim goes, and therefore incalculable and not open to rational debate.

The teachers at psychoanalytical training institutes therefore find themselves in a cleft stick. On the one hand, many of them have learned to present psychoanalysis as something open to rational discussion and to competently put across specialist areas, such as social, cognitive or developmental psychology. They endeavour to use an unequivocal intersubjective language for the theory, and search for a way of judging psychoanalytical competence. On the other, they uphold the metaphorical character of psychoanalytical concepts and insist that the encounter between analyst and patient can never be fully clarified, in other words rendered accessible at the conscious level.

If lecturers at a training institute find themselves in the clutches of this dilemma then the students will also find themselves in a very difficult position. They learn a language that sounds metaphorical and listen to stories about the therapeutic process that are full of allusions. And the students also notice that their teachers themselves tend to think the lectures are describing something objective and unequivocal. It is, after all, highly confusing if a teacher of psychoanalysis reports how he was able to 'contain' the affect of his patient and yet does not intend this report as a narrative full of associations, but instead as a depiction of fact. And it is equally confusing if a teacher (or researcher) speaks about a 'central relational conflict' but denies that this theme of conflict only becomes ambiguous within the subject-based therapeutic relationship.

We cannot hope that this dilemma will be solved. However, psychoanalysts could feel safer in its clutches if they were more keenly aware than hitherto of the dual character of their language and the contradictory nature of their profession.

Things are similar as regards *training analysis*. Here, too, professionalisation has led to a paradoxical situation. On the one hand, the 'post' of training analyst is highly respected, and through his analyses, the training analyst strongly influences the learning process of participants in further training. On the other, the appointment of training analysts is based on subject-based criteria and no light is shed on the tasks associated with his position. It would seem that the institutionalisation of psychoanalysis has generated a high position but has failed to subject this position to public control.

However, this contradictory character goes well with the 'dual function' (Cremerius, 1986, p.1077) which the training analyst has to fulfil at a professional institute. His office and that of the lecturers needs to be given a fixed position in the hierarchy and to be clearly defined. Like any organisation created within an institution, this position will rest on the defence mechanisms of all involved. On the other, *as a training analyst* he is expected to act by perceiving unconscious phantasies in his own conception of reality. This includes being able to question his own participation and the preconditions for the joint undertaking. The current situation is therefore a compromise between two opposing interests: the institution's interest in control over those who hold office within it, and the interest of the training analyst and lecturer in surrendering to the unconscious phantasy in the psychoanalytical process.

In general, we can say that the more a psychoanalytical institution ties its training analysts into its work, gives them tasks and sets them goals, the less scope the analysts enjoy in their psychoanalytical experiences with their analysands.

5.   The Outlook

Would it have been possible to avert the professionalisation of the psychoanalytical profession in order to ensure that it did not contradict the professional ethic? Could psychoanalysts have forgone laying claim to social recognition and material rewards that professionalisation promised? However 'negative' (R. Jacoby, 1975) psychoanalysis was towards society, it could not continue to contradict it in the long run. It gained influence and recognition precisely because its critique of social reality was correct. However, this led to it losing its 'eccentric' vantage point beyond social reality. It had been the thorn in the side of a culture which now integrated and neutralised it[3].

Psychoanalysis would appear to have fallen victim to its own goals – at least at this level of the far-reaching claim to be a method for deconstructing and healing the individual pathology as mediated by social reality. Perhaps, however, the need for social recognition and control already implies a turn toward a new level of independence. To the extent that we can foresee the future today, incorporation into the German Act on Psychotherapy and the regulations for specialist doctors will lead to the profession of the psychoanalyst disappearing as a professional title, too. Forthwith, only specialist doctors (e.g. for psychotherapeutic medicine) and psychological psychotherapists will exist, following the wave of doctors additionally accredited to offer 'psychoanalysis'. Perhaps this will spawn new movements, perhaps groups of psychoanalysts will emerge who will make their scientific and methodological services available to interested persons outside the remuneration system and professionalised training institutions – whether for learning or for personal scholarly exchange. This being the case, it may prove beneficial in the future if at present there is no one who can lay claim to the label of 'psychoanalyst'.

NOTES

[1] In 1915 Freud wrote: 'In other words, can we truly say that the state of being in love which becomes manifest in analytic treatment is not a real one?' (Freud, 1915a, SE vol. XII, p. 168.)

[2] At long last, 'real' exams can be set, where what counts is not the candidate's stance, and certainly not his personal suitability, but knowledge and his aptitude to act correctly.

[3] To put it very polemically: the thorn then became a kind of pimple on the surface.

Helmut Reiff

The Fading Appeal of Psychoanalysis

'The earth is round: You can always keep going left.
By continually pursuing the most extreme, provoking,
innovative idea you go right round and come around
and find yourself back on the extreme right.'
Umberto Eco

Time and Future

We all have our unconscious concepts of reality – concepts which are
also our image of the future. For example, in her essay *Eigenzeit* Novottny (1992, p.51) suggests that the 'future as a linear predetermined
construct comes threateningly close to the future.' It is worth considering
this frequently voiced view more closely, for the confrontation between
the linear infinite time of the future and the finite time of the present
leads precisely to that type of paradox with which Zeno so surprised
people. After all, at what point does the finiteness of the present shift
into the infinitude of the future? Only the image of a circle provides a
way out of this logical trap – the circle is both 'finite' and 'infinite'.
Evidently, here we are at that thin white line where the perspective of
infinite linear progress dissolves and we find ourselves staring fearfully
into the abyss of world doom, or on the way back from it encounter
out-dated horrors and satisfactions we had believed were things of the
past. Yet even if we advance further and go the whole way round we
will always meet the others who have remained behind.

I wish to embark on the following investigation bearing this aspect
of the cycle in mind, one in which the past promises no certainty and
the future promises the return of the past. Incidentally, out of the first
bodily circular movement we develop a movement which completes
itself by returning to its starting-point, which is in fact the very first
image. This is the beginning of a concept of space such as that which

Piaget outlined (1950). This experience of a shape introduces the first order into the world, and it is an order which enables us to re-discover things and thus identify them. In a next step, 'practical' space as generated by our own movement then allows us to experience change in the form of presence and absence, as well as enabling us to experience time as a consequence – the precondition for what we term identity. Just as the physicists construe there being uniform space/time, so, too, in the field of psychoanalysis, we do not utilise *a priori* categories of space and time. Instead, space and time respectively stand for particular experiences and arguments. They should be considered metaphors, similar to those in the dialectic of wish and reality, of feeling and thought, of first and of secondary process.

The wish of the analyst and the dream of the little butcher's wife

Psychoanalysis features the investigation of dreams by means of the primary process. According to Freud, this primary process assumes the role of shibboleth (Freud,1932) which decides whether you are one of the disciples or not.

Let us therefore start with a trial passage from Freud's *Interpretation of Dreams*, namely with the dream of a 'clever' hysterical woman (Freud SE vol. IV pp. 147ff):

'This was the dream:

I wanted to give a supper-party, but I had nothing in the house but a little smoked salmon. I thought I would go out and buy something, but remembered then that it was Sunday afternoon and all the shops would be shut. Next I tried to ring up some caterers, but the telephone was out of order. So I had to abandon my wish to give a supper-party.'

Freud reports the dream in the chapter on distortion in dreams and in connection with his 'psychological explanation' (p.147), which his patients counter with 'remorseless criticism' and 'invariably contradict'.

Before addressing the dream, we therefore hear that the patient contradicted the analyst's wish to prove the wish-fulfilment in the dream. Does a dream really have to do only with being right? We expect a quite different, if forbidden wish, in transference. The fact that the latter wish has been dashed explains the aggression. And the argument about who is right would certainly not have caused the patient to lose sleep and compulsively generated the energy required to produce the dream.

Her dream must achieve both: the first-stage controversy with the analyst, and the fulfilment of her wish.

The manifest dream text is short and striking. At three points the patient tries to fulfil her wish: 'I wanted... I thought... I tried,' and each time she fails because of the realities. At home all she has is a little salmon, the shops are closed, and the telephone is broken. Resignation is the final point in her short and fierce struggle: 'I had to abandon...'

Transposed onto her relation to Freud, she wishes to give the dinner, that is herself, but the erotic ingredients are lacking. At home, all she has are a few preserved bits of salmon – here, desire has evidently been largely consumed. She is prevented from self-gratification. To do so, she would have had to start at an earlier point in time. It is already Sunday afternoon, so there is hardly any time left before her wish will finally be dashed. She places all her hope in the suppliers, i.e. in Freud, but communication with him is disturbed.

Wish-fulfilment in dreams

When Freud suggests that she has tried to attain wish-fulfilment in the dream, then this amounts to rejection by him as regards her dream of wish-fulfilment. It amounts to saying that her only hope is self-gratification. She countenances this possibility, but 'all the shops would be shut'. She remains shut, as does he, too. She would be dependent on his delivery. Nevertheless, Freud is right with his 'psychological expla-nation', for in the mechanisms of the first stage, not only does wish-fulfilment needs to be referred to the dream, but conversely the dream needs to be related to wish-fulfilment. Both are cause and effect. And the quality of sensation in the first stage is also irrelevant: what counts is quantity. The dream has to do with the strong wish which overpowers her during the tranquillity of a Sunday afternoon. As the guardian of her sleep, the dream fulfils this wish by ensuring that wish and wish-fulfilment coincide in the first stage. From the viewpoint of the second stage, the dream has to be inverted in terms of form and contents. It would then read: 'My wish to be taken by Freud is being fulfilled. The bond between us is undisturbed. We have much time and are both quite open. I have his large phallus alone to myself.'

Seen economically, the rejection must tie the bulk of the instinctual energy by transforming the affect in question, for the repression by means of the metaphors of 'supper-party', 'salmon', 'shops', 'caterers', 'telephone' is evidently insufficient on its own.

The associations and the level of metonymy

It was Lacan who made metonymy into a tool for psychoanalysis. Metonymy entails transposing the name of an object onto another object by virtue of the fact that the contents of the two are related at some level, for example in the expression, 'the Crown of England', where the crown stands metonymically for a form of rulership. Lacan took Saussure's theory of the diachronic and synchronic axes in language and applied it to the unconscious. He classified the metonymic, dia-chronic shift as the basis for metaphorical and synchronic concentration. Even if this does not quite do justice to things (cf. Holenstein, 1975, p.154), the distinction does go a long way toward giving the unconscious a systematic form. Incidentally, it also concurs with Black's interaction theory of metaphors, to which we shall return below.

The associations Freud's patient has can thus be construed as the expression of a metonymic shift of the dream contents, as the precon-dition for their metaphoric substance. She first reports on her husband, an 'honest and capable wholesale butcher', who had stated the day before that he 'intended to start on a course of weight-reduction' and therefore 'above all' would 'accept no more invitations to supper'. Her husband was concerned because he was becoming too stout and in need of physical exercise and therefore wished to keep his distance from the seductive enjoyments of company. In other words, in her dream the patient metonymically links her husband's abstinence and the remainder of the salmon (the salmon as metaphor for his reduced state). If he has become stout and refuses to go out, she, too, is forced to forgo pleasure. In her dream she reluctantly identifies with his refusal. What are the consequences of this abstinence? She 'laughingly' adds that her husband had made the acquaintance of a painter who had wished to 'paint his portrait' because of his expressive features. 'Her husband however had replied in his blunt manner that he was much obliged, but he was sure the painter would prefer a piece of a pretty young girl's behind to the whole of his face.'

As in the dream, the butcher's wife comes quickly to the point. Like her husband, she loves calling a spade a spade and, as in the dream, here too she derives her pleasure (laughter) from the rejection. But what is behind her husband's blunt language? In his discussion of the dream, Lacan (1966) identifies immediately with the butcher and dedu-ces from his brash words the great deeds of a 'genital character' (p.216). I believe the butcher's behaviour allows us to propose something else:

If, as the dream suggests and the man's behaviour confirms, we assume that he has no pleasure in sex or is impotent, then his encounter with the painter reveals a homosexual/anal fixation and/or a feminine identification. Evidently, the prior aggressive, vocationally legitimated responses he forms with regard to the anal partial object (the ham) no longer suffice in order to prevent his passive/feminine regression. In the transference, Freud becomes the painter, the butcher's refusal is connected with the analysis of his wife and, in the refusal, both offer themselves to Freud as objects of love. In other words, here the conscious refusal stands for unconscious sexual satisfaction which both wish to obtain from Freud, the painter.

At this point, Freud has difficulty in resisting his patient's invitation – as in the dream she offers herself to him. He does not interpret her suggestion, but helps himself out by resorting to a proven tool: he himself engages in association and borrows an innocent line of identification from Goethe: 'And if he hasn't a behind, / How can his Lordship sit?' The behind thus becomes neutral flesh again, on which one sits. And Freud, the noble man, only wishes to make a picture of things and therefore rejects the invitation to supper.

His patient does not let go of her wish: 'She was very much in love with her husband now and teased him a lot. She had begged him, too, not to give her any caviare.' – And what is this supposed to mean? 'She explained that she had wished for a long time that she could have a caviare sandwich every morning,' but had asked her husband 'not to give her any caviare, so that she could go on teasing him about it.' Irrespective of her husband's abstinence, you will not find caviar, such a delicacy, at a butcher's and the patient therefore returns to her forbidden wish, that of Freud's daily caviar in her sandwich, an 'expense' she 'grudged' herself. Not only in the dream does she transform the necessity of the renunciation she is forced to make through denial into pleasure; she also applies this means forgoing the pleasure of caviar which she affords each day in the form of analysis, and yet does not afford.

At this juncture, Freud distances himself strictly from the proceedings for the third time. This 'explanation' strikes him as 'unconvincing' and her 'reasons' 'inadequate', and somewhat perplexed he therefore asked: 'But why was it that she stood in need of an unfulfilled wish?' 'I pressed her for some more.' The patient, thus rejected 'after a short pause', which Freud believed corresponded to overcoming a resistance, introduced her 'very skinny and thin' friend (whom she had visited the day before) into the equation. She 'confessed she felt jealous' of the friend 'because her husband was constantly singing her praises'. Fortunately, her husband did not desire thin women. The conversation of the two had focused on her friend's wish 'to grow a little stouter. Her friend had enquired, too: "When are you going to ask us to another meal? You always feed one so well." ' Freud now thinks he has clearly identified the motif of the dream: jealousy of the friend who spoils her pleasure at an invitation to supper. The salmon in the dream transpires to be the friend's favourite dish which 'she grudges herself... no less than my patient grudges herself caviare.'

The patient confesses her wishes for love to Freud at three points, namely in the form of the dream, the scene with the painter, and the wish for a caviar sandwich each day – and on each occasion he rejects her. As prophesied in the dream, his shop remains closed, the telephone (i.e. communication) continues to not function properly. The patient now identifies with the skinny, hungry friend who enjoys her husband's 'high opinion': here, we have recognition of renunciation. Via identification with the renunciation, pleasure in anorexia takes the place of instinctual action at the level of oral, anal and phallic partial objects.

Freud readily takes up the identification with the friend and concludes his analysis with it: 'My patient put herself in her friend's place in the dream because her friend was taking my patient's place with her husband and because she (my patient) wanted to take her friend's place in her husband's high opinion.'

Social wish production

Freud ascribes to the patient the more harmless solution entailing jealousy of her friend. The image of the good butcher thus remains unsullied, the patient is shown to be a loyal wife, and Freud has factored himself out of the equation. As he himself so often described, here the analyst flees from the desires of a woman. She transforms the substitute he offers her into pleasure by means of the primary process.

It is legitimate to refer the patient's dream and associations to the analyst's wish for it is he who determines the framework in which wish-fulfilment occurs. His wish for denial necessarily becomes her wish, for only in this transformation does she have a chance of fulfilling her wish.

I am not interested in criticising Freud's approach but merely want to point out how here the struggle is all about wishes and prohibitions. The wish is consequently expressed in a language which leaves it unsatisfied and urges it ever onwards, but also at the same time couches it in safety. Freud is not interested in the disappointment of the butcher's wife, in her narcissistic balance, but in her defence mechanisms. As we know, he counsels renunciation, advising that we trade in the short happiness of instinctual satisfaction in for the security of cultural achievements. The psychoanalyst functions as the advocate of the Ego *vis-à-vis* the instincts and/or the negative side to it, the Superego. Freud patiently undertakes the work of symbolisation in order to reveal the cultural landscape of sublimated 'high opinion'.

Needless to say, the instinctually neutralised Ego is a fiction. Deleuze and Guattari (1972) have shown how the two – Ego and instinct – are interwoven in what is, in the final instance, a no longer penetrable weave. An entire industry is devoted, to use their words, to introducing 'the wish into the mechanism and production into the wish' (p.31).

The ambiguity of their concept of wish production focuses on the so-called natural wish for consumption and satisfactions, a wish that is also socially produced. The distinction between the real, the useful, and the imperatives of nature on the one hand, and the fictitious, the beautiful, and the superfluous of culture, on the other, simply dissolves, i.e. we can no longer distinguish between economic necessities and cultural productions.

In like manner, Bourdieu (1979) proves that the production of culture completely accords with the mechanisms of producing economic goods and, moreover, that production and consumption themselves are homologous in functional and in structural terms. A structural approach thus replaces a focus on contents. In a manner similar to that described by Lévi-Strauss for ethnology, the main thing now is to articulate reliable distinctions and these are, in turn, imperative for all social life. The side effect is that it becomes possible to distinguish between different products for different needs and thus the production of difference itself becomes what is important. This is nothing other than the creation of a language – and it is not possible within it to distinguish between a natural base and a cultural superstructure. Production no longer satisfies a natural need, but itself produces needs. The needs satisfy production and *vice versa*. In this way, what is valuable, what is necessary, and what is healthy all become socially-defined constructs. Through identification with social progress, the external order eventually becomes a natural need. The discovery of nature is thus to be found at the end of the emergence of culture. At the end of the day, the picture of things we had expected is thus completely stood on its head in all respects.

Language also develops in this way, from the primacy of the artificial metaphor to the priority of the natural object to which the word is merely external. In metaphor, wish and word still form a unity. To the extent that language becomes realistic, the metaphor dies. They finally come to be called 'dead' metaphors once they only stand for the reality they once produced but which has since become an independent natural reality.

In his 'interaction theory' of metaphors, Black (1979) describes this process whereby the wish becomes a word from a linguistic point of view. According to him, a metaphor actually consists of two subjects, the primary 'literal' thing or noun, and a secondary characteristic describing this thing. And the two levels are switched round when using metaphors. If Romeo considers Juliet his sun then it is because of her sun-like qualities, which suggest to him the paradoxical noun of the sun for Juliet. In other words, in metaphor something emerges on the surface which would otherwise remain concealed in the unconscious metonymic chain of features common to all concepts, and forms a new concept. In the process, language changes the thrust of the statement, away from some function referring to the object and toward the subject, from the outside to the inside. (Romeo speaks in the metaphor more of his own feelings than of Juliet's objective qualities.) To put it more precisely, in metaphor the distinction between outside and inside, between object and subject, no longer plays a role: they are one. The signifier in the metaphor admittedly points to the signified, but also to its own form and thus back to itself – this paradox has been described quite analogously by Winnicott (1970) with reference to the so-called transitional space in which we create a new reality that was already there. In metaphorical concentration, we switch the logical levels, in other words create a paradox, which, owing to the fact that it dissolves identities and blends different categories, contains the core of the creative and therefore sexual act. Bourdieu (1979) puts things similarly when he says: 'If you wanted to investigate quite precisely what happens in a mind as it develops, when confronted by a new experience, you would be surprised to initially find sexual thoughts' (p.186).

There is an obvious analogy here to the approach taken by psychoanalysis where, by means of transference, the wish and the unconscious sexual link are made. In the case of Freud's patients, this was sublimated to become a metaphorical high opinion. And, in the final instance, this wish appears quite natural.

A Marxist such as Ivan Illich (1977) believes that the power interests of the ruling class are at work in the social production of wishes. Taking the example of medicine, he comes to the well-documented conclusion that medicine causes people to become ill in order to incapacitate them therapeutically and induce conformity (p.140). However, his appeal to the liberated personal responsibility of the mature individual would seem to lead out of the frying pan and into the fire, for, to this end someone would have to define the conditions for such free self-development. What actually happens can be seen in Wilhelm Reich's writings: under the sign of liberated sexuality, of 'the right to a happy life', Reich places instincts under a dictatorship. He not only exposes sexuality to language (or liberates it from its speechlessness), but at the same time sets the definitions for how language is to be used by specifying what counts as healthy and liberated sexuality. His counter-culture therefore immediately becomes a dictatorship of liberated sexuality.

As regards wishes and satisfaction, we could speak of a Marxist and of a capitalist myth. The one claims to know the nature of humankind and human wishes, accords them to suitable satisfactions and deprives them of any inappropriate satisfaction. The latter knows its products, for which buyers – in other words, wishes – have to be created.

In the final instance, any path only goes so far and then turns round again; this is true in psychoanalysis, too. The path leads from the wish to language and from there back to the wish. Freud, after all, did not feel obliged to use concepts such as health, illness, or healing – but fortunately made the primary process the basis for his theory. If we take our initial example, then Freud's wish produces his patient's rejecting dream. Her dream produces a compelling wish for satisfaction by Freud and also his own satisfaction. Her husband denies himself a wish and therefore satisfies another passive/anal wish, the one that is his wife. And the patient uses this satisfaction, in turn, in order to present her wish to the man Freud, who uses it to fulfil his through sublimation.

The destruction of the wish

Psychoanalysis is a language game, the rules of which oblige the 'players' to repeatedly address the wish in the discourse. It is a play of words in which the form of metonyms and metaphors unconsciously combine with one another. We also term this process positive transference. The analyst in his transference function substitutes for the symptom, which appears as the concretisation of the forbidden wish wherever the chain of symbolisations is broken. The analyst resembles a crutch that helps bridge the broken link. Once identification with the function the analyst has thus borrowed has become sufficiently stable, the analysand can let go of the symptom. The process of treatment comes to a standstill, however, if the analyst does not identify with his analytical function as a figure of transference, but introjects the wish which has become real in the symptom and thus triggers a paranoid cycle of projective identification.

We shall not concern ourselves with the first case here. The second, however, bears on the present theme. Let me give an example, if one from another realm, namely from that of the military.

I came upon the following election slogan written on the wall in a Foreign Legion barracks: '*res non verba*'. Words of command which ostensibly command their own abolition, written in the language of command. Admittedly, in them the command of hard facts is juxtaposed to words, but it is nevertheless clear that conversely those who master the words and the (Latin) language also command the facts. And those who receive the commands carry them out. This is a splitting of reality which impairs both parts. Those who command do not 'feel' the effect of their commands on their own bodies; those who act bear no responsibility for their actions. Freud described something analogous in his 'Splitting of the Ego in the Process of Defence' (1940e). The path the wish might take into language is thus blocked and conversely language detached from the body. The wish then projects itself into the body of the listener and finds satisfaction introjectively there through that which the wish encounters in reality. Here, all that would remain of sexuality, which *per se* contains an identificatory element, would be destruction, penetrative, violent, repressive.

Splitting, projection and introjection are not the privilege of the military. They occur wherever language excludes the others. German, traditionally the language of the 'thinkers and authors', was expanded to include that of the journalists, the politicians, the scientists. Language has become a brand-name commodity and claimed rulership for itself. In such a setting, consumers define themselves as the speechless. The consumers' communication consists solely of consumption.

Behaviourism shows us how psychotherapy also becomes something readily consumable and therefore shuts the subjects up. Watson (1919) called for consciousness – that is to say the subjective factor – to be banished 'once and for all' from psychology, and thus initiated the project of psychology as an objective science. Observation took the place of interpretation, and consciousness was replaced by behaviour and social control. Although it was unavoidable that the subject was gradually re-attached to this behavioural apparatus *thereafter*, the primacy of the objective continued to be upheld. With his pithy motto of a 'cognitive turn' Bandura (1979) actually succeeded in creating the artifice of 'cognitive behaviouralism'. He therefore avoided exposing behaviourism as a mere metaphor, in other words as a highly subjective construct (see Bruder, 1993). In psychoanalysis, incidentally, there is a comparable developmental lineage – for the Ego psychology put forward by Hartmann (1964) entails the Ego mutating from a sub-section of the psychological apparatus into a sub-section of the personality.

To all intents and purposes, any number of random therapeutic goals can be tailored to a psyche that has been subjected to this kind of learning theory. Allow me to quote briefly from a course programme for advance training in behavioural therapy: 'This procedure is intended to improve self-perception, the expression of feelings, and mutual understanding, to promote the ability to face conflicts, and to further the development of new, more satisfying opportunities for living together' (TAVT, p.16).

The loss of language in psychoanalysis

Psychoanalysis was always at an advantage compared with behaviourism, for as a theory of the primary process it was always also a theory of language and thus of the subject. However, this language has been caught up in a paradoxical dilemma. Owing to its claim to express the unconscious it has never really been able to hope for anything more than mere toleration in social discourse. Nevertheless, psychoanalysts are increasingly complaining that they are not understood, for example in the current debate on the frequency of sessions.

For example, in connection with the experiences she has made on the role of frequency in the study seminars Gemma Jappe writes (1992, p.17) about the 'increasing resignation in our association over the same period as the idea of three-hour-analysis has won over our members.' 'Could, one must clearly ask, the decline in analysis and the in part rampant opposition to it in its classical setting have to do with the wish to leave in the unconscious that which is perpetuated there awfully in inexorable timelessness (the fascist past)?' 'Admittedly, "orthodox" psychoanalysis encounters difficulties wherever it turns, but nowhere is its systematic exclusion from the catalogue of available therapies being pursued with such bureaucratic and legal perfection as in Germany at present.'

Jappe claims, perhaps rightly, that the fascist past has survived in the unconscious of Germans, for the 'wish' 'to leave in the unconscious that which is perpetuated there awfully in inexorable timelessness' is certainly not just a matter for the psychoanalytical notions of human nature. It may also be that for some decades people have succeeded in preventing this serpent from rearing its ugly head (if not necessarily with the assistance of four hours a week of analysis) and that it is now doing ready to strike. The grandchildren of Auschwitz are at work 'with bureaucratic and legal perfection'. It follows that the 'systematic exclusion' of four-hour analyses 'from the catalogue of available therapies' is nothing other than anti-Semitism.

Moreover, Jappe feels traumatised by the attacks of society on the terms of psychoanalytical treatment. I can understand her arguments – including her feeling personally affected, her identification with the trauma. But things become problematical when, as someone affected, she also adopts an interpretative standpoint, for such a stance would have to rest on a certain degree of abstinence, one that she evidently lacks here.

From a different perspective, what initially seems to be a bitter struggle against reactionary social tendencies turns out to be a home-made problem. For, as empirical studies over the last few years have shown, we analysts are for well-known reasons ourselves in the process of abolishing four-hour analyses. Therapy of a lower frequency is in demand, is socially more practical, and more lucrative. Cremerius (1993) has, moreover, demonstrated that the struggle for the fourth hour rightly side-tracked analysis even more – 'therapy' became the illness which it was supposed to combat.

For this reason, over and above all external dangers and struggles, we should ask what position we take *vis-à-vis* Freud. In our example of a dream we saw him identify with the function of abstinence. What is the state of play as regards abstinence today?

Here, again, a glance at language will help us most. I outlined above how, in the course of social change, metaphors constantly die out and become the maids of external reality – a reality which appears all the more natural to us as a consequence. Wishes are realised through progress. However, the wishes inevitably get lost along the way. Things may be similar with regard to psychoanalysis. Over the decades, a wealth of knowledge has accumulated – the secondary process – and has joined thinking in terms of the primary process. Initially metaphorical terms such as neurosis and narcissism, defence, repression, and the unconscious have lost their metaphorical quality and become the natural reality of our everyday lives. The psyche has been mapped, and its development, its 'bio-psycho-social' contexts, deciphered. Concrete factual knowledge pervades diagnostic work, therapeutic techniques, and even large-scale scholarly projects. With each instance of social recognition, a bit of the primary process gets lost. And our borrowings from academic psychology, as well as the compromises with medicine in the framework of psychosomatics and psychiatry, have also impacted here. In other words, we can point to the dangers which result from social recognition and which consume it internally with at least as much right as those commentators who have pointed to the external dangers which are impairing psychoanalysis.

In the cycle of progress we have thus ended up on the obverse of the circle, on the reverse side whence the original phenomena can only be recognised as such by inversion. Here, the primary process is subordinated to the goals of the secondary process. Trauma and reparation have taken the place of instinct and defence. The wish is no longer expressed, but instead satisfied. One could even maintain that to the extent that psychoanalysis loses its appeal thanks to its concretism in theory and practice, behavioural therapy is discovering the metaphor and thus becoming creative.

Postscript
The primary process and the philosophy of Parmenides

In the primary process, there is neither a diachronic order of time nor Euclidean space. A thing can stand for its opposite or for a third party that is simply related to it. Form and content, part and whole, are identical.

Just as the secondary process asserts itself in an external reality of time and space, so, too, the primary process obeys the rules of language with its concentrations and shifts. Its logic is a grammar which we find both customary and strange. For this reason, we remain unconscious of our thought processes. We cannot say where our thoughts come from and how they are formed. We clutch onto the secondary process by recognising ourselves and the others through the construction of identity in space and time. The secondary process suggests to us that we see an identity in the sense of A = A, whereas the primary process exposes this identity as a mere angle of vision (Bourdieu, 1978).

Construing things similarly to the notion of primary process, Parmenides linked thinking strictly to being and condemned those who assumed that there is non-being as well as being, non-being which cannot and may not be thought at all, and who 'by conflating being and non-being in their thinking, inevitably find themselves in an inextricable web of deception and madness' (Capelle, 1968, p.161). In Parmenides' thought, being is not divisible. It has no beginning and no end, does not evolve or decay, knows of no motion. Thought and the object of a thought are one and the same. Parmenides breaks with our familiar picture of the world and challenges us to face thought with no secure standpoint, no identity, no time as fixed regularity.

One should desist from over-hastily pointing to the lack of a logical distinction between time and space, for disproving things by means of the secondary process causes as many logical problems as it solves, as Parmenides' pupil Zeno showed with his famous paradoxes. How can you divide infinite space into finite parts? How can something move and yet also be located at a particular point? How can one think nothingness? Modern physics is evidently starting to bond more with Parmenides than with Aristotle.

However, by means of the logic of the secondary process we construct – or rather the ego does – a reality by means of the concepts of identity and denial that evidently stands the test and enables us to plan and act reliably. In this reality, the things which constitute the world have their place, and their duration. Nevertheless, this thought does not assume the truth of space and time. Instead, the categories of space and time presume the concept of truth. In other words, we must turn our argument round. What is decisive is not that reality as experienced proves this thought to be true, but that it itself produces the truth, that the concept of truth only makes sense in categories which this philosophy has established.

In the primary process there is no truth, not even that of the wish. But only in the primary process can we think the wish as the difference which makes life worth living. Let us hope that this difference remains upheld for us in psychoanalysis, too.

Michael Wirsching

Psychotherapy in Upheaval

*Ecological Change En Route
to A Different Modernity*

Preliminary Remark – Thesis

'Psychotherapy in upheaval' is an ambiguous topic. Alongside changes in psychotherapy itself, what comes to mind are personal and social crises in which treatment should be applied. Let us start with the most pertinent question: When do people go to a psychotherapist? As a rule, not until there seems to be no way out of their situation in life. If questions and conflicts crowd in upon them and become insurmountable, they look for outside help. This is all the more likely to happen if symptoms have already arisen. They may be the expression of excessive strain: depression, disturbed sleep, a greater likelihood of falling ill, to name but the most frequent and most unspecific. Others are already the expression of unsuccessful attempts at self-healing, the consequences of conflict solutions that have gone wrong: fear avoidance through phobias which impair the normal pursuit of life; compulsive rituals which place life in tight chains; anorectic hunger strikes, or compulsive eating. In all cases, the symptoms cause suffering and yet are intended to make something that is tolerable even worse. Other people are regularly involved, and today we even talk of a system of problems. This includes the patient, the family, the 'helpers' and whoever else forces their way in or may belong within the system, or has been drawn in. We all know the system's own attempted solutions. Well-meant advice, a trip to the GP, days or nights spent discussing things, and much more besides. The participation of one therapist, or of several at once, is a relatively new variant for solving psycho-social conflicts, but it is growing in significance.

People, families, or entire systems may stand the test of lengthier periods of time despite larger inner or external strain. One precondition for this is that those concerned maintain the feeling that something can somehow still be done, that there is a way out, that there is still hope. By contrast, we also see that once everything is in flux, once helplessness and hopelessness have spread out in chaos, even everyday and highly familiar causes may trigger crises. We speak of catastrophes if quantitative change ('more of the same') switches over into qualitative structural change.

The notion of upheaval is more idiomatic, less a reference to a pathology, and free of the theoretical premises of chaos theory. In other words, psychotherapy is sought out in times of personal, family or social upheaval. It then endeavours to keep the necessary self-organisation (what Maturana [1985] and Luhmann [1984] termed *autopoiesis*) on a favourable track. As part of the system, psychotherapy itself is subject to upheaval if the underlying conditions for it change. If the cognitive, methodological or economic conditions for psychotherapy change, then there will inevitably be disturbances in its development.

The thesis I wish to pursue in the following remarks is therefore as follows: We are seeing how psychotherapy is sought out during times of personal and general upheaval. In this way it contributes to the development of the individual and society. However, in the process it finds itself caught up in the swirl of currents that can be catastrophic, indeed, in the classical sense of the word, may thus culminate in a decisive and final turn for the worse. Is psychotherapy the expression of a new form of thought and a contribution to new thinking – or is it an overdue attempt to halt the decline, and thereby an obstacle on the way to fundamental reconstruction? That is my question.

I shall try and assess my thesis by considering the change in the social setting, in the theories and methodology of psychotherapy, and the most recent attempts to secure the basis for the profession. The goal is to take critical stock at the end of Modernity.

Psychotherapy – an eye-catching phenomenon en route to a different Modernity

Psychotherapy is a product of the Enlightenment, with its roots in the Romantic medicine of the 18th century – although the concept first occurs at the end of the last century in England, France and Holland (Schott, 1986). Seidler (1990) has recently pointed out that around the turn of the century psychotherapy already underwent upheaval with the turn away from Mesmer's magnetism and hypnosis – as a consequence of Sigmund Freud's 'discovery of the unconscious' as the key determinant influencing the formation of psychological symptoms (Ellenberger, 1973). We can discern three phases of ever-accelerating development, each phase being embedded in developments specifically in the scientific world-view. As with any historical process, the different terms are by no means clearly marked off from one another. Instead, the old and the new often exist unlinked side by side, either long term or until one of those legendary paradigmatic leaps triggers off fundamental change (Kuhn, 1970).

In other words, such a paradigmatic shift occurred at the beginning of the development that concerns us here, namely the farewell to metaphysics and the advent of modern psychotherapy. The assumption that something was dynamically repressed and that its unconscious effect could be exposed in order to offer humans a better understanding of their conflicts and thus a more conscious basis for decision-making and developing further (where Id was, Ego ought to be) has left its mark on psychotherapy to this day. This critical and hermeneutic paradigm underlying psychoanalysis has ensured that the depth-psychologically orientated schools have to this day enjoyed the sympathy and support of progressives, and, starting with the Nazis, have attracted the persecuting hatred of the oppressors and stupefiers of men the world over. Psychoanalysis is a highly esteemed companion of the major enlightening and liberating movements of Modernity. At the same time, two trends have been its undoing, which, introduced by its founder, at first strongly fostered the development of the discipline and then were also the two main causes of its equally rapid decline. What I mean is firstly what Jürgen Habermas (1973) has termed the scientistic misunderstanding psychoanalysis had of itself. For it wished to be not only a cultural anthropology, but also a recognised treatment providing healing that was thus indebted to the natural sciences of the 19th century. Such an insistence on the medical aspects came to a pathetic end in American psychiatry some 20 or 30 years ago, when it was swiftly and thoroughly expelled from the centres of science and medical power. The second fateful heritage has been the fact that psychoanalysis has ignored its original principles (enlightenment and emancipation) when designing the basis for itself as a profession, in particular when training new psychoanalysts, a fact to which Cremerius (1987), Parin (1981), and most recently Ortega (1991) have most energetically pointed.

Orthodoxy and sectarianism, grotesque calls for sacrifice and material egotism have caused a loss of respect for the psychoanalytic profession in Germany, too, which to this very day makes it repugnant to those favourably inclined toward psychoanalysis – and permits its opponents to triumph.

The second developmental step following on from the psycho-analytical revolution at the turn of the century was to occur in the 1950s during the 're-building' of German society. In a period during which guilt and injury were repressed and the Cold War broke out, the inimical blocs entered into a dull clinch that escalated symmetrically. The majority was by no means interested in emancipatory enlightenment. The order of the day was not to contemplate, to reflect on oneself, to expose hidden conflictual structures, but instead swift, cool and above all efficacious action – a trend the Mitscherlichs (1967) described as an inability to mourn. Developments in Europe followed the general trans-Atlantic drift. American behaviourism and the rapid growth in clinical psychology – with consulting and counselling services – were gaining in influence. Countless studies in behavioural therapy, and they were often based on laboratory experiments, indicated superiority with regard to combating symptoms. Such positive psychotherapy became more up-to-date and more effective. It obeyed the generally recognised rules for empirical science.

The protest movement of the 1960s, led by students and adolescents, initiated a third developmental stage – in the shape of a classic counter-movement. Established psychotherapy, which was somewhat dry, technical and petty in outlook, was washed away by a psycho-boom, by a veritable proliferation in methods and fashions. Difficulties arose as regards the difference between truly liberating experience or, to use Herbert Marcuse's phrase (1965) repressive de-sublimation, and true upheaval or playfulness, with the sides opting either for *tichy-touchy* or for New Age. Meanwhile, some 300 to 400 'treatment schools' confirm a strong interest and growth potential.

Today, in the run-up to the turn of a new century and our entry into a new millennium, the mood has calmed somewhat but conditions have by no means become less murky. On the contrary, the new obscurity (Habermas, 1985) has become a true sign of the times and psychotherapy is now truly in the middle of the fray. There is hardly an area of life, a phase of life, or a life crisis that is not at least potentially a target for some form of psycho-social intervention. To draw on another of Habermas' images, what we see is truly an almost complete colonisation of the lifeworld or, to put it with somewhat less pathos: psychotherapy has become everyday.

Life today expects a great ability to integrate and solve conflicts – of both the individual and society. Individuals can, if they so wish, design their lives and bear responsibility for them themselves – indeed, this is necessary. Social scientists speak of individuation and the informalisation of the life-worlds. This results from the dissolution of socially binding canons (Hassan, 1988). Dogmas and salvation theories are no longer on the agenda. What they are after – whether true or not – are mental constructs which are readily interchangeable – or so Heinz von Foerster (1985) would have it, the computer engineer currently so influential in family- and hypnotherapy as well as psychosomatics. What is actually 'real' becomes ever more impenetrable in an age of perfect media-based simulations (Baudrillard, 1988). We take part in everything, and in nothing. In an essay published shortly before his death, Friedrich Dürrenmatt (1991) reminded us that as early as 1911, Vaihinger had, in his study *Philosophie des Als-Ob*, investigated a question that is so topical now, namely 'how, despite knowingly employing false conceptions, we nevertheless attain to the truth'. Our theories determine our observations, or so Einstein would have it, in the wake of Goethe's dictum which stipulates athat even looking at nature already creates a theory. The lifeworlds have changed. It is no longer simple to predict the phases in the family cycle. Sequential monogamy prevails. Living singly, with a partner (in wedlock), with children (perhaps from different relationships) – the sequence of constellations is subject to infinite variation, both in the life of the individual and that of society (Beck & Beck-Gernsheim, 1990). Not only the individual, but the entire system is challenged. What we face are bonds that are too strong, or too unreliable, intractably opposed to one another or at deadly harmonic peace – and the risks are immense. The 'system' is, as always in history, ideal for decisive, predominant groups. Today, we are accommodating the cunning, youthful, dynamic, assertive type with his love of life. Learning to perceive and accept our own and social boundaries is something that entails effort and pain, and comes at the price of irreversible destruction. One has to seek out social support and justify it in each individual case. No one starves here, no one is openly persecuted because of their beliefs. We are not oppressed, just depressed, or so postmodern philosopher Jean Baudrillard (1989) would have it in his *Cool Memories*. And André Glucksmann (1991) also concludes that Europe is depressed. Depression, chronic helplessness and hopelessness, a lack of subjectively perceived social support – all of these add up to shortened life expectancy, as we have known ever since Schmale & Engel (1967) published their findings. A lack of social support is, for example, more of a risk to health than is smoking, or so the US medical sociologist House found in his survey published in *Science* in 1988. The way we suffer psychologically or physically is largely determined by inherited genes, viral infections, the strain posed by the environment, and life styles. However, whether and when we fall ill and what course the suffering takes is something decided by psychological, family and social factors. Illnesses are not some fate randomly spread across the population, but negative cycles which emerge at those social, family, and biographical flash-points. Illness-inducing living conditions, for example, chronic lack of help and hope, also undermine a return to health, and troubles which have not been overcome become additional burdens for patient and for family. People try almost despairingly to counter this by always bringing the same strategies for solution – which are quite unsuitable for solving fundamental things and only offer short-term respite. We need to broaden the perspective here: in a society which is as strongly in upheaval as is ours, maintaining identity in chaos becomes a life-long task for every one of us. If the development of fundamental trust-fostering psychological structures continues to be denied during earliest childhood, if the ability to clarify and solve conflicts is not catered for, and if highly-differentiated cultural demands are met with primitive simulation strategies ('acting as if'), then disturbances in experience and behaviour are inevitable. If people hardly discuss, feel, or overcome the inevitable challenges of everyday life, then these will tend to threaten their already fragile identity. Adopting readily interchangeable stereotypes, conforming to actual or ostensible external expectations may bring short-term internal peace, but in the medium term it does not help. This explains the immense range of neurotic and psychosomatic disturbances – by far the most widespread form of suffering in our society (Schepank et al, 1987).

In this dire situation, medicine has become a dominant discipline. However, that version of medicine which is one-sidedly geared to the natural sciences is clearly not up to handling the plethora of tasks or meeting the wealth of expectations. It is, as it always was, a synopsis of biological, psychological, family, and social viewpoints.

The demand for psychotherapeutic help is accordingly growing steadily. People are looking for self-encounter, the clarification and solution of conflicts, aids in communication and interaction, access to opportunities for decision-making and personal development in situ-ations which are log-jammed, a helpful trusting relationship, maturation with a correcting, new emotional experience. And all of this is on offer. The key fits the lock. Psychotherapy is one of today's most striking inventions. It is both attempted solution in a socio-cultural crisis and a game of relationships, a further simulation of fundamental human experiences, a highly complex, iridescent entity at the end of Modernity.

As a next step, let us look at how psychotherapists prepare themselves in terms of theory and methodology in order to be able to do justice to this cultural role.

Theory and the crisis in methodology in the 1990s – reluctant integration or the preservation of diversity

For many years, the main controversy was between psychotherapists who took their cue from critical hermeneutics, Enlightenment and emancipation, on the one hand, and those schools which focused on objective science, that is to say Popperian positivism, on the other. Today, the struggle of psychoanalysis versus behavioural therapy has lost much of its edge. After a truce based on a desire to uphold the peace within the profession (as both parties had a stake in the health insurance system), other debates would also appear to have waned. Instead, we have seen a quite explosive spread of 'alternative' psycho-products and ensuing chaos. A powerful counter-current is arising, as is the case in other domains of culture and science affected by the new obscurity. The universal theories which many thought had been lost following the end of the Vienna circle of thinkers – theories which wished to equip physics, biology, chemistry and above all the humanities with a common epistemology, language, and methodology – are now celebrating a Renaissance. Above all, systems theory, constructivism, and semiotics claim such a role for themselves.

Two sub-sections of psychotherapeutic medicine occupy the leading positions in this debate, namely family therapy and psychosomatics. This is hardly surprising as both – and they interact in complex ways – tackle quite impenetrable systems: the family, on the one hand, and the bio-psycho-social complex that determines illness, on the other. Re-placing mechanical causal chains with systemic networks would indeed seem to be a highly persuasive approach, whereby self-organisation (*autopoiesis*) engenders more and more new entities at various levels (emergences). In a new, so-called second-stage cybernetic system, in the place of a closed circuit of rules there is systemic openness. When the therapist, for example, enters the scene this in itself creates a changed situation. The latter can be varied in terms of form and content depending on the specific school of thought the therapist follows. This insight has put research into psychotherapy in recent decades into a state of suspense (Garfield & Bergin, 1986). Starting from a comparative assessment of the results of different procedures (termed the 'horse-race design' by analogy with prescription testing), via meta-analyses of the effective power of thousands of studies of treatment (Smith et al, 1980), what has remained below the line is the oft-cited statement from *Alice in Wonderland* which Luborsky (1975) quotes: All have won, and all must have prizes. In other words, psychotherapy in general achieves effects more positive than one might assume from a spontaneous situation. A third of the respective disturbances is usually improved substantially by most of the procedures tested, one third records satisfactory results, and one third remains unchanged or deteriorates. Imparting an in-depth understanding of conflict, the quality of the therapy relationship, and the acceptance of the patient's attempt at self-healing are all key factors for success over and above all schools and studies. There can be no insight without a trusting relationship to the therapist, there can be no development without an expanded understanding of the disturbance, and there can be no enduring success without recognising the patient's own endeavours to solve the problems.

An even 30-30-30 spread of the results of treatment will no doubt not just give statisticians cause for second thoughts. The absurdity of the dictum 'psychotherapy is effective' first becomes manifest if, following Grawe (1989), we compare it with the pronouncement 'medicine is effective'. Imagine we wished to base our medical system on an approach which linked all kinds of physical ailments to all kinds of medicines, surgery, physical therapy or other forms of treatment – we would perhaps arrive at similarly coincidental favourable or unfavourable results. It is also conceivable that depending on the syndrome chosen at random, differing basic approaches would be favoured. In one case, those in favour of surgical intervention would prove superior. In another, the victors would be those advocating pharmacotherapy. Indeed, even the outsiders would be sure of booking an occasional success and therefore justifying the slice of the health insurance cake they claimed for their own. Now let us imagine that the different schools were to complete utterly different forms of training. One camp would study chemistry or biochemistry and would then attend evening courses where they would learnt to prescribe medicines. Another would perfect certain manual skills in a master's workshop. A third group would be physicists who would be able to explain and use radiation apparatuses. This scenario gives us a relatively good picture of the current crisis in psychotherapy which takes the form of a totally bogged down argument about various schools and method.

Allow me to make use of a second comparison. However complex the biological processes of life and however complicated the ways in which they are disturbed, and however multifarious the theories, methods, and treatment systems promulgated by that section of medicine which is based on the natural sciences, all of this rests on a fundamental paradigm of natural science. Things are similar as regards the psychological processes, which are based in a culture, society, personal biography and the dynamics of personal relationships, not to mention their disturbances. And the theories, methods, and systems of treatment advanced by psychotherapeutic medicine are likewise highly differentiated. In other words, we incontrovertibly need a psychotherapeutic system for our epoch and society which is as differentiated as university medicine and treats just as broad a spectrum of tasks. Now, and here things get really complicated, university medicine and psychological medicine must be linked – as our patients cannot be intrinsically divided. We need not create new mini-groups and mini-schools around each new idea or clinical discovery. The narcissism of minor differences is counter-productive. From the outset, neither psychoanalysis nor behavioural therapy nor system therapy, let alone any other variant, is better or more accurate than any of the others. What is actually new is precisely the diversity. And the whole is the false, to quote Adorno.

This adage alludes to the need for structural change, for a willingness to rethink and re-organise things. As a point of fact, there are growing signs that we are in the midst of a renewed period of upheaval. At the beginning of the century, as stated, the first, psychoanalytical revolution occurred in psychotherapy, giving it scientific foundations. This triggered fruitful developments as regards concepts and methods. Today, the three most powerful streams – depth psychology, learning theory, and systems theory – concern themselves not with major theoretical projects, but with standard scientific 'tidying up' operations. They are linked in that they all assume there is a causal connection between symptoms and psychological processes. They all set great store in the changing impact of verbal interventions, of the 'talking cure', as Bertha von Pappenheim (Anna O.) called it when talking with her physician

Josef Breuer, one of Sigmund Freud's mentors (Breuer & Freud, 1895). All three main currents consider the helpful relationship of therapist and patient to be a necessary if not intrinsically sufficient basis for successful treatment. They thus all differ fundamentally from magical rites and from scientifically-based biological interventions. In the conscious perception of these mutually-linked foundations lies a strong formative power. Then, the conscious acceptance and cultivation of diversity can take the place of some harmonising craving for integration or, better, conformity. Starting from the fundamental psychotherapeutic paradigm, the order of the day must be to do justice to the differences between people and their cultures, their specific needs and conflicts as well as the quite individual disturbances that these engender. We must also take into account the diversity of underlying social and economic conditions. And, finally, the idiosyncrasies of the people who act as psychotherapists, their different world views, experiences in life, and interests must all be taken seriously.

With this second revolution in psychotherapy we must bid farewell to an approach to medical treatment centred on the individual and the search for the one true psychotherapy. Instead, we must recognise diversity, forms of interaction, and the creative possibilities open to human life.

The renowned biologist Jakob von Uexküll (1928) has taught us that humans and the human environment (a term he coined) are inextricably and reciprocally related and therefore generate ever new shapes and forms. The whole is more than the sum of its parts. In this regard, he became a pioneer of the ecological thought so necessary for our survival today. For this reason I shall call the current revolution, the current structural changes in psychotherapy, its 'ecological change'. As with any instance of something fundamentally new penetrating minds, no one today can really imagine that things were ever really different. Orthodoxy, reformation movements, attempts to evoke a unified therapy, etc. are all only of historical interest, that is, unless they are seen in a new overall context.

Professionalisation – regional association instead of sectarianism

Let us finally address the practical consequences of the trends I have outlined. This is important because the diversity I have called for can also lead to chaos. Where do the patients seeking help, the trainees, and the politicians responsible for the framework of rules find guidelines? We need to know at this point where and how doctors – together with psychologists one of the two main professional groups discussed here – work in psychotherapy and what standards their abilities have to meet.

First of all, there is the area of so-called basic care. A rhetorical question: Can we approve of a doctor, particularly one working on his own, who is not able to take into consideration the emotional aspect of a physical illness, to advise the patient accordingly himself, to recognise the necessity of beneficial specific psychotherapy, and, if necessary set the patient in the right direction as regards such treatment? Over the next few years we will continue to focus on the present across-the-board efforts to establish truly useful training[1]. The main preconditions for this must have been laid before graduation, and study courses must consequently be redesigned in the institutes and nation-wide. Far-reaching psychotherapeutic abilities in the narrower sense are to be recommended as a supplement to the various specialist medical fields. The pioneers here are the child and adolescent psychiatrists. In 1989 they made psychotherapy an obligatory part of their training courses. In comparison, only about half of the general psychiatrists active in Germany are deemed to be competent. Nevertheless, it seems hard to imagine a long-term future in which psychiatrists do not have qualifications in psychotherapy. It is also conceivable that we will see an increase in the number of general practitioners, specialists in internal medicine, neurologists, paediatric doctors, gynaecologists, dermatologists and others who have acquired the necessary skills to be able to work by truly combining psychotherapeutic and psychosomatic insights. In the future, given the wealth of tasks that cannot be delegated and intensive training in the natural sciences, why should psychosocial skills not be an obligatory component in any qualification as a specialist physician?[2].

A word on the development of psychoanalysts, or to be more precise on the additional title of psychoanalyst, is in order here. In the future, this qualification should be officially given a higher status and brought into line with the internationally recognised level at which it is already taught in most institutes. Real psychoanalysts should be trained here, freed from the onus of having to acquire psychotherapeutic or even specialist medical skills. We simply cannot dispense with such trained persons when it comes to the treatment of severe chronically disturbed personalities and as experts who can be trained to act as supervisors and training therapists, not to mention the indispensable role they would play in the scholarly development of the field.

A specific location itself requires a group of specialists, however. Students wishing to become full-time medical and psychological psychotherapists are currently receiving a broad range of theoretical and methodological skills in only a few places, mainly at universities. It is obvious that with so many applications, skills must be duly and professionally acquired and further developed somewhere if the entire system is not to suffer a drop in standard. What we need are experts who understand something of the field. It will be they who press scholarly advances ahead in order to bridge the growing gap between research and practice. Within the treatment system, they will handle the very complicated chronic cases which require co-ordinated and often combined treatment. The lack of specialist doctors for psychotherapeutic and psychosomatic medicine is obstructing developments, as is the lack of specialist psychologists.

The wealth of tasks mentioned could be anchored in regional academies. In an association that upholds the independence of the groups concerned, doctors and psychologists, psychoanalysts, behavioural therapists and family therapists could then work together in university and extramural institutions. The psycho-social system that is fragmented into professional groups, schools and other interests would be replaced by a regional federative association, which interweaves the research tasks and the development of theories and methodologies, as well as the further training tasks necessary to foster the profession's identity.

A second, clearly ecological change in psychotherapy

Let us return to our starting point. *En route* into a different Modernity (Beck, 1986), we are experiencing the dissolution of the canon and the dogmas, the individualisation of what are now informal lifeworlds. There is a growing awareness of how we are determined by biological, psychological and social interdependencies in which we are embedded. As a result, each individual now faces tasks which involve handling conflicts, shaping social relations, and recognising and accepting limits, something that can easily over-strain people. Individual and social solutions, however widespread they may be, become the main problem if they do not involve a complete re-think. High-tech and video wars are only another miserable instance of what is always the same. For the individual person, the collapse in bodily, emotional, and social forces

127

engenders chronic biological, psychological and social disturbances if it is not countered at an early stage by a turn away from the old and now useless pseudo-solutions by means of help that is geared to the patients and personal development.

Beyond all positivistic ideologies of normality or health, the upheaval in our society calls for a paradigmatic shift in psychotherapy. In the second developmental leap a century after that taken by psychoanalysis, psychotherapy has again caught up with the ongoing upheaval in our world-view and has, in part, contributed to the change in it. In what we have termed an ecological change, humans are now seen as embedded in their environment. Nature, the psyche, relationships, and society are all part of a whole. We intervene in the interaction between them with the goal of creating the preconditions for more favourable development.

Psychotherapy is a part of our social system which is currently in a state of flux and has important evolutionary tasks. In its full breadth and diversity, psychotherapy has become an everyday matter, in the truest and best sense of the word.

NOTES

[1] Such fundamental diagnostic and consultative abilities on the part of psychologists is quite indispensable, for example for work at a job centre, as a school psychologist, or a traffic psychologist.

[2] At the psychologists' end, comparable qualifications are expected of staffers working in counselling. Psychologists working in prisons or in the school service should receive the opportunity for further qualification similar to the additional title specialist doctors have acquired. Designing such further training courses is far from easy.

Martin Wangh

Doubting the Future of Psychoanalysis

Toward the end of the 1960s and through to the mid-1970s, the psychoanalytical community, at least in the United States, seemed to be deeply pessimistic with regard to the future of psychoanalysis. Anna Freud herself made remarks to this effect in a lecture which she gave in 1968 in New York and which was attended by a large number of American psychoanalysts[1]. She derived her sombre assessment mainly from what she considered an attitude of animosity toward history and introspection which she discerned among the rebellious youth of that decade, a generation which felt 'history and the past' as well as 'law and order' to be 'irrelevant' or a regressive obstacle to emotional freedom and human progress. Kurt Eissler was likewise pessimistic as regards orthodox psychoanalysis in its pure form.[2]

In 1974, the APA's Program Committee decided to address this mood of concern in the form of two panel discussions to be held in the spring and autumn of that year. The one was to consider 'the future prospects of psychoanalysis' from a critical *inside* perspective, the other to approach the same issue *from the outside*. The panel for the first discussion consisted solely of APA members, while some of the speakers at the second session came from other (academic) fields. In what follows I shall mainly focus on the deliberations of the second panel discussion.

Before summarising the opinions of these 'outside' critics and presenting my own opinions on the issue of the future of psychoanalysis, I would like to make a few historical observations on the external events and the development of psychoanalysis at that time.

In the late 1920s and early 1930s, the theoretical range and clinical horizon of psychoanalysis increased immensely. The 'Superego's' origins and energies were outlined and with the publication of Anna Freud's *Ego and the Mechanisms of Defence* (1936) psychoanalysis moved a good step closer to clarifying the Ego function. At about the same time, Heinz Hartmann placed Ego psychology and the problems of adaptation at the centre of research[3]. His perspective expanded thinking on the Ego functions to include a teleological dimension.

This widening of the sweep of psychoanalytical thought in the clinical and theoretical domains led to psychoanalysts swiftly taking a leading role in military psychiatry when, at the beginning of the Second World War, all manner of psychologically traumatised victims had to be treated. At least among the Western Allies, psychoanalysis' clinical conceptions sidelined once and for all the psychiatric notions dating back to the days of the First World War of simulated and/or male hysteria and similar diagnostic categories. Psychotherapy took the place of the pointless electro-convulsive therapy or punishment. The image of a rational, positive science attracted a large number of young medical officers. Thus, immediately after 1945, the growing number of psycho-analysts were highly optimistic, and this optimism spilled over into the entire population. Many patients with symptoms endeavoured to obtain psychoanalytic therapy. Conversely, there was a change in the type of pathologies for which psychoanalytical consultation was recommended. The 'scope' of psychoanalysis seemed to have widened.[4] Moreover, with the strengthening democratic mood world-wide, broader sections of the population felt entitled to lay claim to medical care and this specifically included treatment for psychological suffering.

As early as the War years, the pressure exerted by this demand for therapy had led to various versions of psychoanalytically-based group therapy for soldiers; now, these variants were extended to the population as a whole. In comparison, psychoanalysis proper, i.e. the classic one-to-one treatment setting, was reserved for a relatively small number of patients.

In the course of time, psychoanalysis was also provided for patients whose pathology was closely bound up with their character structure as well as for cases somewhere on the borderline between psycho-neurosis and psychosis. The disillusionment with treatment which was prompted by this expansion went hand in hand with the social dis-appointment which, as mentioned, surfaced in the pessimistically coloured proclamations of the youth of the 1960s.

Following this detour into the history of psychoanalytical theory and practice I shall now return to the 1974 panel discussion on the Future Prospects of Psychoanalysis – considered from the outside. I will limit myself here to giving a brief summary of the remarks of three speakers there.[5]

Ilya Wachs, professor of comparative literature at the exclusive Sarah Lawrence College not far from New York City encountered among his students the same disinclination to learn and the same resistances as those which Anna Freud had bemoaned in her 1968 lecture to psychoanalysts. His students, he reported, felt alienated and were passive; they treated their bodies as if these were some external, mechanical objects that could be switched on or off. They were ostentatiously concerned with their own metabolisms, with nutrition and excrement alike. Finding and preparing special food took up a large part of their time. They fled from the feeling of being integrated human beings and accordingly also ran away from any confrontation with themselves in the framework of psychoanalytical treatment. Frequently, they had been robbed of any protective and stabilising family environment owing to their parents' divorce. Wachs read their regressive behaviour as a defence mechanism against an overwhelming fear which was closely linked to the fear of the destruction of all humanity either by a nuclear war or by an ecological catastrophe. He called on psychoanalysis to counter this panic, to recognise the social problems that thus arose, and to consider them one root of the resistance it encountered. It was not sufficient, he opined, only to bemoan these counteracting forces.

Carl E. Schorske, professor of history at Princeton University, was a man who was especially well versed in the intellectual history of *fin de siècle* Vienna and he started his 'reflections on the future of psychoanalysis' by remarking that the three major thinkers of the 19th century, namely Hegel, Marx and Freud, had all hoped that reason would in the final instance prevail over human irrationality. Nevertheless, he continued, all three had failed with their attempts to familiarise us with a rational world. Hegel had believed that humanity would recover from the irrationality of the French Revolution; Marx had expected that the repression of the individual brought about by the Industrial Revolution would be overcome by class struggle; and Freud had hoped that his discoveries would enable people to enjoy their sex lives and individual freedom. Psychoanalysis, Schorske maintained, had not attained this goal owing to the ever more pronounced decline of the nuclear family. 'The rule of Narcissus takes the place of the Oedipus complex.' Given these conditions, psychoanalysis, he averred, must change its rationally oriented treatment techniques and goals if analytical therapy were to be successful. More empathy and intuition were needed to help the individual suffering from his narcissism.

Quite apart from this fact, Schorske claimed, concern for the individual, the epitome of 19th century humanism, was itself brought into question. This was especially true of Eastern Europe, the Far East, China, and Vietnam, where the majority of people lived under Communist rule. There, Kohut's call for a new approach and an empathetic attitude on the part of the analyst would inevitably go unheard. What was important was to improve the psychological situation of the masses, not the state of the individual. In short, Schorske gave psychoanalysis hardly any chance of surviving, unless it reduced the rational and scientific claims it made and focused more strongly on the more mystic and intuitive links between the analyst and the patient.

Robert L. Heilbronner, an economist who was the most active participant in the discussion, viewed the future of psychoanalysis quite gloomily. Like Schorske, he believed that civilisation would develop in the direction of peasant communism on the Chinese model. He assumed that all of humanity would eventually live in some sort of monastic order, with one uniform belief, achievement-oriented in terms of behaviour, and without any space for individualistic reference to the self, such as the psychoanalyst fosters and presumes. He doubted whether psychoanalysis would be able to adjust sufficiently to survive in such a climate and to bring its humanising thrust to bear. Admittedly, psychoanalysis was to a certain degree the diametrical opposite of the dialectical thought of communism. However, while communism believed that humans could be formed positively, psychoanalysis discovered an *immutable, intransigent* reality determined not by culture but by biology. As *theories*, both taught that ambiguity had to be accepted – in contrast to the above-mentioned practice whereby a 'monastic order of rulership demands uniformity and unequivocality'. 'Psychoanalysis was a laboratory to investigate human nature; that is its achievement.' By placing themselves in the service of this task, the privileged few who can afford analysis pay off their debt to humanity. To Heilbronner's mind, the crowning achievement of psychoanalysis would be if it succeeded in discovering and promoting a 'universally shared conception of correct behaviour' acceptable to all cultures. Psychoanalysis, he suggested, should enlighten us on the core of what he then termed 'moral precepts' for everyone.

It is quite striking that Heilbronner and Schorske, both of whom are pessimistic as regards the future of psychoanalysis, nevertheless by way of a goal and a hope uphold the idea that psychoanalysis is the main source of a rational existence and should show us the path to a 'universal morality'. And Kurt Eissler, the pessimist among the analysts, to a certain extent joined forces with these critics.

Ironically, clinical psychoanalysis today, twenty years after the panel discussion in question, faces a mixture of political and economic currents in the capitalist world which severely impair its free ability to work. While Western capitalism showers the greatest praise on individualism and has made 'privatisation' its battle cry, psychoanalytical treatment and dynamic psychotherapy are beyond the financial means of the average citizen. The fact that a health insurance company has to assume the costs of the psychotherapeutic treatment has led to this third party, because it foots the bill, intervening and disturbing the basic precondition that are essential for maintaining a trusting, open and constant relationship between psychotherapist and patient.

In the United States today, so-called 'health maintenance organisations' with which a person in gainful employment has to be insured if he wishes to apply for a course of treatment, dictate how often and how long a patient will receive psychotherapeutic treatment. These anonymous organisations demand the submission of reports diagnosing the illness and stating the progress made in the healing process, and such reports decisively violate the trust of communication between doctor and patient during analysis.

Let us ignore for the moment whether or not it was the wide number of treatment methods for psychotherapy which arose with the spread of psychoanalytical thought which was damaged by the development of psychoanalytical knowledge. We can at any rate state that the materialistic, capitalist source of disturbance poses the key threat to psychoanalysis today. Psychoanalytical research in the strict sense is no longer possible, as its 'test material', namely the patient, is no longer able to pay for the treatment and health insurances are not prepared to assume the costs of treatment on the scale necessary. Given these circumstances, it is not possible to maintain the optimal framework for research, that is, the classic one-to-one setting. Psychoanalytical research is back where it started in the early years, when the number of patients was very small. Thus, psychoanalytical insights can only be gained from treating either an elite group of highly affluent clients or an elite of resolute patients and analysts themselves willing to make financial sacrifices.

However, we must nevertheless ask whether these conditions must indeed signal the end of psychoanalytical research, the demise of psychoanalysis, the end of its efforts to bring a highly refined method to bear in order to find an understanding for how the human psyche functions. After all, it does so in the context of an analytical situation which must remain undisturbed by external attempts to intervene, must guarantee confidentiality, and in which regular treatment sessions must be ensured in order to allow free association to flow without external obstacles.

In his 1969 article, Kurt Eissler assumed that psychoanalysis in the classic analytical sense had exhausted its potential for insights and had come up against its limits. I do not believe this is true. Not only can we deepen our knowledge of the development of the human psyche by directly observing mother-child interaction and also arrive at new insights through research into brain functions, but a careful study of transference and in particular of counter-transference affords a constantly growing crop of new insights. Moreover, the different forms of therapy that have arisen out of psychoanalysis – group therapy, family therapy, diverse forms of movement therapy – also provide psychoanalysis with new knowledge that can be brought to bear in the classic one-to-one setting. The process is definitely reciprocal: while the therapeutic descendants feed off classic psychoanalysis, they at the same time generate a keener awareness for what the patient narrates in the classic analytical scenario about his everyday encounters and conflicts in his family reality and elsewhere. In addition, we learn to observe how patients and analysts are equally affected by tension in the social and political worlds.

The mushrooming of these various new therapies evidently also has a negative side to it. They attract a large number of patients who would otherwise have been suited for an intense course of psychoanalytical treatment. Furthermore, the widespread use of psychotropic medicines in the case of psychological disturbances also lowers the number of such patients. All these treatment variants impact most severely on the training of future psychoanalysts. Owing to the dearth of patients seeking analysis, prospective candidates now find it harder to acquire experience on the job.

Despite these obstacles, psychoanalytical instruction is blossoming, as today there are more training analysts available at more places. I should qualify this by saying that the number of medically-trained candidates is contracting steadily. However, we can assume that the stable, balanced future development of psychoanalysis is assured given that it is being taught at an ever greater number of places and institutions, not to mention the fact that, in the form of journals printed in a variety of languages, an ever denser network of communications channels now exists spanning the earth. Moreover, if we bear in mind how the number of people world-wide with access to Western thought, philosophy and civilisation has grown, then the potential number of persons who might seek out psychoanalytical treatment has probably grown as a ratio of the world population.

In view of the economic pressure which I have already mentioned, as well as the unification of semi-alternative forms of therapy and chemical forms of treatments, I do not believe that psychoanalysis as a form of treatment can expect to lose its elitist status in the near future. This should not be taken to mean that psychoanalysis as a science and a treatment method has come up against its limits. We should get used to the fact that its training institutes, candidates and researchers should be considered analogously to the wide-ranging R&D departments in industry. Psychoanalysis should lay claim to precisely this status in societies.

What future psychoanalytical research must offer is a range of ever more exact observations on how the human mind functions (or rather the soul, meaning the mind and emotional life), observations on somatic reactions to psychological and physical stimuli, insights into the formation and spread of morals, on ethnic characteristics, and on many other facets of human action, too. We must learn to notice and describe a great many more things than hitherto. These can be achieved by drawing on technical means that expand our perceptual faculties, for example using audio-visual, computer-assisted recording apparatuses which are already available or which we need to develop. And all this, of course, costs money. In order to secure the requisite financing, psychoanalytical research must be considered as if it were any other field of R&D. To this end, psychoanalysis must ensure that it attracts the attention and interest of public and private institutions that finance research. It must not shy the limelight if it wishes to gain public recognition as an area of R&D.

In her inaugural address on the occasion of the foundation of the Sigmund-Freud chair at the Hebrew University in Jerusalem, which was read out in her absence in 1977.[6] Anna Freud spoke (just as I did in my lecture on the same occasion) of the necessity of bringing together the efforts of all social scientists and biologists, including psychoanalysts, and pooling their work in an Academy of Human Studies (to use Kurt Eissler's term). Such united efforts are needed if we are to find a way of constraining human aggressivity. The human death wish is currently threatening to destroy the very biosphere of our earth and with it, of course, human life. It is an unconscious instinct and to date only psychoanalysis has developed some rudimentary ways of dampening the forms in which it manifests itself and establishing what channels must be left open to direct it away from its goal. Only by gaining as comprehensive an understanding of human motives as possible can we help to secure the continued existence of humanity in the face of its own self-destructive proclivities. We know that the forces which form the counterweight to Thanatos reside in the human libidinous potential. It is therefore an equally pressing task to free these creative-sublimating forces from everything which unconsciously prevents them from blossoming. So the question is not whether psychoanalysis has a future. Mankind is dependent on psychoanalytic help if it wishes to have a future at all.

NOTES

[1] Anna Freud, 'Schwierigkeiten der Psychoanalyse in Vergangenheit und Gegenwart,' in: *Die Schriften der Anna Freud*, vol. IX, (Frankfurt, 1987), pp. 2481-2508.

[2] Kurt Eissler, 'Irreverent Remarks about the Present and the Future of Psychoanalysis,' in: *International Journal of Psychoanalysis*, 50 (1969), pp. 461-71. See page 462: 'Although the therapeutic applicability of this method has been extended during the last decades, psychoanalysis as a therapy nonetheless does not have a bright future.' And page 468: 'I would conclude from this that all that can be learned by way of the couch Freud had already learned.'

[3] Heinz Hartmann, 'Ich-Psychologie und Anpassungsproblem,' (1939) reprinted in *Psyche*, 10 (1960), special edition, (Stuttgart, Klett, 1970).

[4] Leo Stone, 'The Widening Scope of Indications for Psychoanalysis,' in: *Journal of the American Psychoanalytic Association*, 2 (1954), pp. 567-94.

[5] Printed copies of the lectures are to be found in the APA archive and I also possess copies.

[6] Anna Freud, 'Antrittsvorlesung für den Sigmund-Freud-Lehrstuhl der Hebräischen Universität, Jerusalem,' in: *Die Schriften der Anna Freud*, vol. X, op. cit., pp. 2907-15.

Biographical notes on the contributors:

Johannes Cremerius, born 1918. MD, Professor Emeritus of Freiburg University. Specialist in psychiatry and neurology, and internist. Teaching analyst – German Psychoanalytic Association. Numerous articles in journals.
Books: *Die Beurteilung des Behandlungserfolges in der Psychotherapie* (Heidelberg: Springer 1962); *Die Prognose funktioneller Syndrome* (Stuttgart: Enke 1968); *Zur Theorie und Praxis der Psychosomatischen Medizin* (Frankfurt am Main: Suhrkamp 1978, italian edition, Boringhieri); *Vom Handwerk des Analytikers* (2 vols, Stuttgart: Frommann-Holzboog 1984, italian edition, Boringhieri).
Editor: *Die Rezeption der Psychoanalyse in der Soziologie, Psychologie und Theologie im deutschsprachigen Raum bis 1940* (Frankfurt am Main: Suhrkamp 1981); *Neurose und Genialität* (Frankfurt am Main: Fischer 1970); *Psychoanalyse, Über-Ich und soziale Schicht* (München: Kindler 1979).

Helmut Dahmer, Prof. Dr., born 1937; teaches sociology at the Darmstadt Institute of Technology. From 1968-1991 he edited the psychoanalytic monthly *Psyche*. Since 1981 editor of annotated edition of the *Writings* of Leo Trotzki (currently 3 vols, in 8 parts, available).
Published titles: *Libido und Gesellschaft* (1973, expanded second edition 1982); *Politische Orientierungen* (1973); *Psychoanalyse ohne Grenzen* (1989); *Pseudonatur und Kritik* (1994); *Divergenzen* (1995).
Editor: Leo Trotzki, *Schriften über Deutschland* (1971); Sándor Ferenczi, *Zur Erkenntnis des Unbewußten* (1978); *Analytische Sozialpsychologie*, 2 vols (1980); Leo Trotzki, *Denkzettel* (1981).

Jürgen Körner, Prof. Dr., born 1943. Diploma in Psychology, psychoanalyst. Professor for Social Pedagogy at the Institute for Infant-, Adult- and Social Pedagogy, University of Berlin. Emphasis in research and publications on psychoanalytic methodology and theory of psychoanalysis, psychoanalytic paedagogy and Balint groups.
Monograph: *Vom Erklären zum Verstehen*, Göttingen: Vandenhoeck und Ruprecht 1985.

Ludger Lütkehaus, PD, Dr., born 1943, visiting professor at several American and German universities. Lives in Freiburg im Breisgau as freelance publicist. Numerous publications on literature, philosophy and the psychology of the 18th - 20th centuries.
Recent publications: *Dieses wahre innere Afrika. Texte zur Entdeckung des Unbewußten vor Freud* (Frankfurt am Main 1989); *O Wollust, o Hölle. Die Onamie - Stationen einer Inquisition* (Frankfurt am Main 1992, italian edition Milano 1993); *Philosophieren nach Hiroshima. Über Günther Anders* (Frankfurt am Main 1992); *Die Schopenhauers. Der Familien-Briefwechsel* (Zürich 1991, italian edition, Palermo 1994); *Arthur Schopenhauer. Der Briefwechsel mit Goethe und andere Dokumente zur Farbenlehre* (Zürich 1992); *Hegel in Las Vegas. Amerikanische Glossen* (Freiburg im Breisgau 1992); *Kindheits-vergiftung* (Editor, Freiburg im Breisgau 1994); *Unfröhliche Wissenschaft* (Marburg 1994); *Schöner meditieren* (Marburg 1995). Editor of the first Schopenhauer edition based on latest manuscript versions (6 vols, 4th edition, Zürich 1995). Special prize of the Schopenhauer Society, 1979.

Rainer Marten, Prof. Dr., born 1928 in California. Professor of philosophy at Freiburg University, with emphasis on Greek philosophy, philosophy of the 20th century and practical philosophy. Joint interdisciplinary work on linguistics, psychoanalysis and theology.
Recent works: *Der menschliche Tod. Eine philosophische Revision* (Paderborn 1987). *Der menschliche Mensch. Abschied vom utopischen Denken* (Paderborn 1988). *Denkkunst. Kritik der Ontologie* (Paderborn 1989); *Heidegger lesen* (München 1991); *Lebenskunst* (München 1993).
Essays on the relationship between philosophy and psychoanalysis: 'Menschliche Wahrheit' in S. Goppert (ed.), *Die Beziehung zwischen Artzt und Patient. Zur psychoanalytischen Theorie und Praxis* (München 1975); 'Versuch über die philosophische Bestimmung des Gewissens' in H. Holzhey (ed.) *Gewissen? Philosophie aktuell*, Vol 4 (Basel/Stuttgart 1975); 'Philo-sophische Überlegungen zur psychoanalytischen Situation' in *Zeitschrift für klinische Psychologie und Psychotherapie* 26 (1978); 'Bemerkungen zur Positivität des lebenspraktischen Nicht' in G. Jappe/C. Nedelmann (eds.) *Zur Psychoanalyse der Objektbeziehungen* (Stuttgart-Bad Cannstatt 1980); 'Die psychoanalytische Situation und der Augen-Blick' in S. O. Hoffmann (eds.) *Deutung und Beziehung. Kritische Beiträge zur Behandlungskonzeption und Technik in der Psychoanalyse* (Frankfurt am Main 1983).

Helmut Reiff, MD, born 1947. Psychiatrist and psychoanalyst (German Psychoanalytical Association), also in private practice. Head of Psychosomatic Clinic at the Kohlwald Clinic in St. Blasien. Publications refer particularly to semiotics, metapsychology and psychoanalytic psychosomatics.

Martin Wangh, MD, Psychiatrist, New York Psychoanalytic Institute and Israel Psychoanalytic Institute. Clinical Professor Emeritus, Albert Einstein College of Medicine, Bronx, New York.

Main publications: 'Day Residue in Dream and Myth', in *Journal of the American Psycho-Analytical Association* 7 (1959); 'Psychoanalytische Betrachtungen zur Dynamik und Genese des Vorurteils, des Antisemitismus und des Nazismus' in *Psyche* 16 (1962) 5; 'Die Mobilisierung eines Stellvertreters' in *Psyche* 17 (1963) 9; 'Die Herrschaft des Thanatos. Über die Bedeutung der Drohung eines nuklearen Krieges und der Einfluß dieser Drohung auf die psychoanalytische Theoriebildung', in Carl Nedelmann (ed.), *Zur Psychoanalyse der nuclearen Drohung* (Göttingen 1985); *Working Through of the Nazi Experience in the German Psychoanalytic Community.*

Michael Wirsching, Prof. MD, born 1947 in Berlin. Succeeded Johannes Cremerius as Professor for Psychotherapy and Psychosomatic Medicine in Freiburg/Breisgau. Psychoanalyst and Family therapist. Assistant physician under Walter Bräutigam at the Heidelberg Psychosomatic Clinic until 1975, subsequently senior consultant, and doctorate under Helm Stierlin at the Research Department in Psychoanalytic Foundations and Family Therapy, Heidelberg University, until 1980; thereafter Professor for Clinical Psychosomatics at the Centre for Psychosomatic Medicine, Justus-Liebig-University, Gießen, until 1989 (Horst-Eberhard Richter). Since then medical director of the Department for Psychotherapy and Psychosomatic Medicine at the University Clinic Freiburg.

Numerous books and articles, with particular reference to family therapy involving severe and chronic physical diseases. Chairman of the German Study Group on Family Therapy, and Commitee member of the German Board for Psychosomatic Medicine.

Bibliographies

JOHANNES CREMERIUS

Alexander, F. *(1957), Psychoanalysis and Psychotherapy,* New York.
— and S. T.Seleneski *(1965),* 'Freud-Bleuler, Correspondence', in: *Archive of General Psychiatry* 12, pp. 1-9.
Appy, J. G. (1986*),* 'Selbstentfremdung der Psycho-Analyse in der Gesundheitspolitik'. *DPV-Arbeitstagungsbericht,* p. 13-30.
Balint, M. (1947), 'On the psychoanalytic training system,' in: *Primary Love and Psychoanalytic Technique,* Stuttgart *1966.??*
— (1958*),* 'Sandor Ferenczi's last year', in: *International Journal of Psycho-*Analysis 39, pp. 68-70.
Barande, R. (1975*),* 'Quels psychanalystes. Et pour quel faire', in: *Revue française de Psychanalyse* 39, pp. 225 -246.
Basch, M. F. (1991), 'Die Zukunft der psychoanalytischen Methode', in: *Zeitschrift für psychoanalytische Theorie und Praxis,* Sonderheft, pp. 2.-5. Bergeret, J.et al. (1987*),* 'Enquête sur la pratique psychanalytique', in: *Revue française de Psychanalyse* 4, pp. 1245-1268.
Bernfeld, S. (1952), 'Über die psychoanalytische Ausbildung', in: *Psyche* 38 (1984), pp.437-459.
Bertin, Celia. (1982), *Marie Bonaparte. A life,* London, Quartet 1983
Bird, B. (1968), 'On candidate selection and its relation to analysis', in: *International Journal of Psycho-Analysis* 49, pp. 513-526.
Braun, K. F. (1992), 'Die gegenwärtige Ausbildungssituation in der DPV im Spiegel einer Umfrage bei den Kandidaten des psychoanalytischen Institutes Heidelberg-Karlsruhe', in: *Psychoanalyt. Info,* No. 38, April, pp. 3-14.
Clark, R. (1979), *Sigmund Freud,* Frankfurt am Main.
Cooper, A. M. (1984), 'Psychoanalysis at one hundred: Beginning of maturity', in: *Journal of the American Psychoanalytic Association* 32, pp.245-267.
— (1990), 'The future of Psychoanalysis', in: *Psychoanalytic Quarterly* 59, pp. 177-196.
Cremerius, J. (1979), 'Robert Musil. Das Dilemma eines Schriftstellers vom Typus "poeta doctus" nach Freud', in: *Psyche* 33, pp. 733-772.
— (Ed.) (1981a), *Die Rezeption der Psychoanalyse in der Soziologie, Psychologie und Theologie im deutschsprachigen Raum bis 1940,* Frankfurt am Main.
— (1981 b), 'Freud bei der Arbeit über die Schulter geschaut. Seine Technik im Spiegel von Schülern und Patienten', in: U. Ehebald und F. Eikkoff (Ed.), *Humanität und Technik in der Psychoanalyse. Jahrbuch Psychoanalyse,* Beiheft Nr. 6, Bern-Stuttgart-Wien, pp. 123-158.
— (1986), 'Spurensicherung. Psychoanalytische Bewegung und das Elend der psychoanalytischen Institution', in: *Psyche* 40, pp. 1063-1081.

— (1987), 'Der Einfluß der Psychoanalyse auf die deutschsprachige Literatur', in: *Psyche,* 41, pp. 32-54.
— (1989), 'Lehranalyse und Macht', in: *Forum Psychoanalyse* 5, pp. 190-208
— (1990a), 'Die hochfrequente Langzeitanalyse und die psychoanalytische Praxis. Utopie und Realität', in: *Psyche* 44, pp. 1-29.
— (1990b), 'Sigmund Freud'. Rundfunksendung im Süddeutschen Rundfunk am 10 Mai 1988. Published in: B. Schultz (Ed.), *Es ist ein Weinen in der Welt,* Stuttgart.
— (1992a), 'Der DPV-Analytiker als Teilnehmer an der Kassenregelung', in: *Forum Psychoanalyse* 8, pp. 63-76.
— (1992b), 'Die Zukunft der institutionalisierten Psychoanalyse', in: M. Kuster (Ed.), *Entfernte Wahrheit. Die Endlichkeit der Psychoanalyse,* Tübingen pp. 63-84.
— (1993), 'Dichter auf der Analysecouch', in: B. Götz, O. Gutjahr und J. Roebling (Eds.), *Das verschwiegene Ich,* Pfaffenweiler, pp. 9-22
Edelson, M. (1988), *Psychoanalysis. A theory in crisis,* Chicago/London.
Eissler, K. R. (1965), *Medical Orthodoxy and the Future of Psycho-Analysis,* New York.
— (1969), 'Irreverent remarks about the presence and the future of Psychoanalysis', in: *International Journal of Psycho-Analysis* 50, pp.461-471.
— (1974), 'On some theoretical and technical problems regarding the payment of fees for psychoanalytic treatment', in: *International Revue of Psycho-Analysis* I, pp. 73-101.
Eitingon, M. (1925), 'Geschäftsprotokoll', in: *Internationale Zeitschrift für Psychoanalyse* 11, p. 516.
Erdheim, M. (1987), 'Wenn Institutionen ver-enden', in: Psychoanalytisches Seminar Zürich (Ed.), *Between the Devil and the Deep Blue Sea,* Freiburg i. Br.
Erikson, E. H. (1957), 'The first analyst', in: *Freud and the 20th Century,* New York.
Fonagy, P. (1993), 'Working together with the President. Thanks at the end of J. Sandler's term of office as President' in: *IPA-Newsletter,* Summer issue, pp. 9-10.
Franzen, S. (1982), 'Editorial', in: *Council for the advancement of psychoanalytic education* 2, p. 2.
Freud, A. (1938/1950), 'Probleme der Lehranalyse', in: *Max Eitingon in Memoriam,* Jerusalem 1950, pp. 80-94.
— (1966), 'The ideal psychoanalytic institute: a utopia', in: *Bulletin of the Menninger Clinic* 35 (1971), pp. 225-239.
— (1972), *Schwierigkeiten der Psychoanalyse in Vergangenheit und Gegenwart,* Frankfurt am Main.
— (1976), 'Bemerkungen über Probleme der psychoanalytischen Ausbildung', in: *Die Schriften der Anna Freud,* Bd. 10, München 1980, pp. 2805-2810.
Freud, S. (1910d), 'The Future Prospects of Psychoanalytic Therapy', SE Vol. XI, p.141
— (1916/19I7 [1915-17]), *Introductory Lectures on Psycho-Analysis,* SE Vols XV & XVI
— (1919a), 'Lines of Advance in Psycho-Analytic Therapy', SE Vol. XVII, p.159
— (1923a [1922]), ' Two Encyclopaedia Articles ', SE Vol. XVIII, p.235.
— (1924f [1923]), 'A Short Account of Psycho-Analysis', SE Vol. XIX, p.191
— (1925d [1924]), 'An Autobiographical Study', SE Vol. XX, p.3.
— (1926e), *The Question of Lay Analysis,* SE Vol. XX, p.179.

— (1933a [1932]), *New Introductory Lectures on Psycho-Analysis,* SE Vol. XXII, p.3

— (1941 [1921]), 'Psycho-Analysis and Telepathy', SE Vol. XVIII, p.177

Fromm, E. (1970), *The Crisis of Psychoanalysis,* New York.

Fürstenau, P. (1994), 'Neue Lebensformen erfordern neue psychotherapeutische Orientierungen', in: P. Buchheim, M. Cierpka, Th. Seifert (Ed.), *Neue Lebensformen – Zeitkrankheiten und Psychotherapie.* Berlin-Heidelberg-New York, pp. 1-12.

Gaddini, E. (1984), Changes in psychoanalytic patients up to the present day., in: R. S. Wallerstein (Ed.), *Changes in Analysis and in Their Training. International Psychoanalytic Association Monograph series* 4, pp. 6-19.

Glover, E. (1937), 'Die Grundlagen der therapeutischen Resultate', in: Internationale *Zeitschrift für Psychoanalyse* 23, pp. 42-50.

Graf, M. (1942), 'Reminiscence of Professor Sigmund Freud', in: *Psychoanalytic Quarterly* 11, pp. 465 -476.

Greenson, R. R. (1967), *Technique and Practice of Psychoanalysis,* Hogarth Press 1966.

Groen-Prakken, H. (1981), 'Die Psychoanalyse in den Niederlanden - Opfer wirtschaftlicher Depression', in: *Bulletin der Europäischen Psychoanalytischen Föderation* 17, pp. 105-107.

— (1984), 'Regierung und psychoanalytische Ausbildung', in: *Bulletin der Europäischen Psychoanalytischen Föderation* 23, pp. 101-109.

Hamburg, D. (1967), 'Report of the committee on central fact-gathering data of the American Psychoanalytic Association', in: *Journal of the American Psychoanalytic Association* 15, pp. 841-861.

Hofmannsthal, H. von/C.J.Burckhardt (1956), *Briefwechsel,* ed. C. J. Burckhardt, Frankfurt am Main.

Holder, A. (1984), 'Psychotherapie und staatliches Gesundheitswesen in England', in: H. Bach, U. Ehebald und J. Weigelt (Eds.), *Psychoanalyse, Psychotherapie, Öffentlichkeit,* Göttingen.

Holt, R. R. (1990), 'A perestroika for renewal psychoanalysis. Crisis and renewal'. Unpublished paper, given on 12 January 1990 in New York; quoted in: A. D. Richards, 'The future of psychoanalysis. The past, present and future of psychoanalytic theory', in: *Psychoanalytic Quarterly* 59, pp. 347-369.

Jacoby, R. (1983), *Die Verdrängung der Psychoanalyse oder der Triumph des Konformismus,* Frankfurt am Main. 1985.

Jappe, G. (1983), 'Bemerkungen über die Probleme der psychoanalytischen Ausbildung', in: S. O. Hoffrnann (Ed.), *Deutung und Beziehung,* Frankfurt am Main, pp. 219-227.

Jaspers, K. (1950), *'Zur Kritik der Psychoanalyse', in: Rechenschaft und Ausblick. Reden und Aufsätze,* München 1951, pp. 221-230

Jones, E. (1953-1957), *Sigmund Freud: Life and Work,* 3 Vols., Hogarth Press.

Joseph, E. (1979), Contribution to the Haslemere Conference 1976, unpublished; quoted in J. Klauber, 'The identity of the psychoanalyst', in: *Sigmund Freud House Bulletin* 3, pp. 5-9.

Kernberg, O. (1984), 'Changes in the nature of psychoanalytic training, structure of the training and standards of the training', in: R. S. Wallerstein (Ed.), *Changes in Analysts and in Their Training. International Psychoanalytic Association Monograph series* 4, pp. 56-62.

— (1993), 'Aktuelle Probleme der Psychoanalyse', in: *Bulletin der Wiener Psychoanalytischen Vereinigung* I, pp. 5-21.

— (1994), 'Der gegenwärtige Stand der Psychoanalyse', in: *Psyche* 48, pp.15-46.

Klauber, J. (1980), Die Identität des Psychoanalytikers', in: *Schwierigkeiten in der analytischen Begegnung.* Frankfurt am Main 1980.

Klüwer, R. (1980), 'Der Einfluß von Theorie und Praxis der Psychotherapie auf die psychoanalytische Ausbildung'. Bericht über die 10. Standing Conference on Training, London 1978, und den Pre-Congress, New York 1979.

Knight, R. (1953), 'The present status of organized psychoanalysis in the United States', in: *Journal of the American Psychoanalytic Association* I, pp. 197-221.

Kohut, H. (1969), 'Forschung in der psychoanalytischen Ausbildung. Ein Memorandum', in: *Psyche* 25 (1970), pp. 738-757.

(1973), 'Die Zukunft der Psychoanalyse', in: *Die Zukunft der Psychoanalyse,* Frankfurt am Main, 1975, pp. 7-27.

Kubie, L. K. (1956), *Psychoanalyse ohne Geheimnis,* Reinbek.

Kulm, T. S. (1967), *Die Struktur wissenschaftlicher Revolutionen,* Frankfurt am Main 1972.

Kuster, M. (Psychoanalytisches Seminar Zürich) (Ed.) (1993), *Entfernte Wahrheit. Von der Endlichkeit der Psychoanalyse,* Tübingen.

Langer, M. (1986), *Von Wien nach Nicaragua,* Freiburg i. Br.

Leeuw, P.J. van der (1978), ' "Modern times" und die Berufsausübung des Psychoanalytikers in der heutigen Zeit', in: S. Drews et. al. (Ed.), *Provokation und Toleranz,* Frankfurt am Main, pp. 42-56.

Limentani, A. (1986), 'Presidential Address. Variation of some Freudian themes', in: *International Journal of Psycho-Analysis* 67, pp. 235-243.

Little, M. (1991), 'Über die Bedeutung von Regression und Abhängigkeit', in: *Psyche,* 45, pp. 914-930.

Lohmann, H. M., und L. Rosenkötter (1982), 'Psychoanalyse im Hitlerdeutschland. Wie war es wirklich?', in: *Psyche* 36, pp. 961-988.

Loch, W. *(1974),* 'Der Analytiker als Gesetzgeber und Lehrer. Legitime und illegitime Rollen?', in; *Psyche* 28, pp. 431-460.

McLaughlin, F. (1967), 'Addendum to a controversial proposal. Some observations on the training analysis', in: *Psychoanalytic Quarterly* 36, pp.230-247.

Meerwein, F. (1978*),* Die Identität des Psychoanalytikers', in: *Zeitschrift für psychosomatische Medizin* 8, pp. 29-44.

Menninger, K. A., und P. S. Holzmann (19 5 8), *Theorie der psychoanalytischen Technik,* Stuttgart 1977.

Merton, K. R. (1949), *Social Theory and Social Structure,* Glencoe/Ill. 1962.

Morgenthaler, F. (1965), 'Mitteilung von Dr. Ph. Sarasin an Dr. Morgenthaler', in: *Bulletin der Schweizerischen Gesellschaft für Psychoanalyse* 1, p. 7.

Parin, P. (1978a), *Der Widerspruch im Subjekt,* Frankfurt am Main.

— (1978b), 'Warum die Psychoanalytiker so ungern zu brennenden Zeitproblemen Stellung nehmen. Eine ethnologische Betrachtung', in: *Psyche* 32, S. 385-399.

— (1986), 'Die Verflüchtigung des Sexuellen in der Psychoanalyse', in: Psychoanalytisches Seminar Zürich (Ed.), *Sexualität,* Frankfurt am Main.

— (1990), 'Die Beschädigung der Psychoanalyse in der angelsächsischen Emigration und ihre Rückkehr nach Europa., in: *Psyche* 44, pp. 191-202.

Peck, M. W. (1940), 'A brief visit with Freud', in: *Psychoanalytic Quarterly* 9, p. 206.

Popper, K. R. (1942), *The Open Society and Its Enemies,* RKP, 1966.

Pulver, S.W (1978), 'Erhebungen über die psychoanalytische Praxis 1976. Tendenzen und Konsequenzen', in: *Psyche* 38 (1984), pp. 63-82.

Roazen, P. (1975), *Freud and his Followers.* Interview with Eva Rosenfeld on 3.9. 1965 and 3. 11. 1966, Bergisch-Gladbach 1976.

Rotmann, M. (1988), 'Der Einfluß von Häufigkeit und Dauer der Sitzungen auf die Entwicklung eines kurativen psychoanalytischen Prozesses. Referat der Tagung der Europäischen Psychoanalytischen Föderation', in: *Bulletin der Europäischen Psychoanalytischen Föderation,* Nr. 31, Herbst 1988, pp. 151-164.

Sachs, H. (1930), 'Die Lehranalyse', in: *Zehn Jahre Berliner Psychoanalytisches Institut,* Wien, pp. 53-62.

— (1945), Freud, Master and Friend, London; Imago, 1945.

— (1947), 'Observations of a Training Analyst', in: *Psychoanalytic Quarterly* 16, S. 15 7- 16 8.

Sandler J. (1983), 'Die Beziehung zwischen psychoanalytischen Konzepten und psychoanalytischer Praxis', in: *Psyche* 37, pp. 577-595.

— (1989), 'Psychoanalyse und psychoanalytische Psychotherapie. Das Problem der Abgrenzung', in: *DPV-Info* Nr. 5, April 1989,

— (1990), 'Die Zukunft der Psychoanalyse', in: U. Streeck und H. V. Werthmann (Ed.), *Herausforderung fur die Psychoanalyse,* München pp. 37-50.

— (1991), 'Mitteilungen des Präsidenten: Prof. Joseph Sandler', in: IPA *Newsletter* XXII, Nr. 2, January 1991, pp. 1 -3.

Smirnoff, V. (1988), *Bulletin der Europäischen Psychoanalytischen Föderation,* Nr. 31, Herbst 1988.

Speier, S. (1983), 'Gedanken zur Ausbildung oder Wie man Analytiker wird', in: H. M. Lohmann (Ed.), *Das Unbehagen in der Psychoanalyse. Eine Streitschrift,* Frankfurt am Main, pp. 104-110.

Steiner, R. C. (1985), 'Some thoughts about tradition and change arising from an examination of the British Psychoanalytic Society's controversial discussions (1943/44)', in: *International Review* of *Psycho-Analysis* 12, pp. 27-71.

Stepansky, P. E. (Ed.) (1989), *Margaret Mahler,* München.

The San Francisco Psychoanalytic Institute (Ed.) (1990/91*), Training Program in Psychoanalysis,* San Francisco.

Thomä, H. (1991), 'Ideen und Wirklichkeit der Lehranalyse. Ein Plädoyer für Reformen (I & II)., in: *Psyche* 45, pp. 358-433 and pp. 481-505.

— and H. K. Schele (1985), *Lehrbuch der psychoanalytischen Therapie.* 2 Vols., Vol. 1: *Grundlagen,* Berlin/Heidelberg/New York/Tokyo.

Wallerstein, R. S. (1986a), *Forty-two Lives in Treatment,* New York.

— (1986b), 'Psychoanalysis as a science: A response to new challenges', in: *Psychoanalytic Quarterly* 55, pp. 44-451.

— (1988), 'One Psychoanalysis or many?' in: *International Journal* of *Psycho-Analysis* 69, pp. 5-21.

— and E. M. Weinshel (1989), 'The future of Psychoanalysis', in: *Psychoanalytic Quarterly* 58, pp. 341-371.

— (1991), 'Psychoanalytic education and research: a transformative proposal', in: *Psychoanalytic Inquiry* 11, pp. 196-225.

Winnicott, D. W (1974), *The Maturational Processes and the Facilitating Environment,* London, Hogarth Press, 1965.

BIBLIOGRAPHIES

Wittenberger, G. (1987), Von der Selbstregulation zum Prüfungskolloquium', in: *DPV-Arbeitstagungsbericht*, pp. 135-144.

Ludger Lütkehaus

Binswanger, L. and S. Freud (1992), *Briefwechsel* 1908-1938 , (Frankfurt/Main).

Cremerius, J. (1994), 'Das psychoanalytische Gespräch,' in: *Das Gespräch. Poetik und Hermeneutik* , XII, (Munich), pp. 171-82.

Freud, S. (1910d), 'The Future Prospects of Psychoanalytic Therapy', SE Vol. XI, p.141

— (1915), 'The Unconscious'. SE Vol. XIV, p.159

— (1926e), *The Question of Lay Analysis,* SE Vol. XX, p.179.

— (1927), 'The Future of an Illusion,' in: SE Vol. XXI, pp. 1-56.

Habermas, J. (1973), *Kultur und Kritik*, (Frankfurt/Main).

Lifton, R. J. & E. Markusen (1992), *Psychologie des Völkermords. Atomkrieg und Holocaust* , (Stuttgart).

Lütkehaus, L. (1989), *'Dieses wahre innere Afrika'. Texte zur Entdeckung des Unbewußten vor Freud* , (Frankfurt/Main., reprinted Hamburg 1995).

— (1992a), 'O Wollust, o Hölle'. Die Onanie – Stationen einer Inquisition , (Frankfurt/Main).

— (1992b), Philosophieren nach Hiroshima. Über Günther Anders, (Frankfurt/Main).

— (1995), 'Verchromte Sirenen, herostratische Apparate. 'Desiderat Dingpsychologie', (G. Anders). Für eine Umorientierung der Psychologie,' in: *Psyche*, 49, No. 3, pp.281-303.

Mann, Th. (1936), 'Freud and the Future,' in: *Essays of Three Decades* London, Secker & Warburg, pp. 411-421.

Pfister, O. (1928), 'Die Illusion einer Zukunft. Eine freundschaftliche Auseinandersetzung mit Prof. Dr. Sigmund Freud,' in: *Imago* , 1928, pp.149-84.

Jürgen Körner

Beland, H. (1983), 'Was ist und wozu entsteht psychoanalytische Identität?' in: *Jahrbuch der Psychoanalyse*,15, pp. 36-67.

Bleger, J. (1968), 'Die Psychoanalyse des psychoanalytischen Rahmens,' in: *Forum Psychoanalyse* 9, pp. 268-80.

Cremerius, J. (1986), 'Psychoanalytische Bewegung und Psychoanalyse als Institution,' in: *Psyche*, 40, pp. 1063-91.

— (1992), 'Der DPV-Analytiker als Teilnehmer an der Kassenregelung,' in: *Forum Psychoanalyse*, 8, pp. 63-76.

Daser, E. (1991), 'Der Integrationsbegriff in der Psychoanalyse,' in: *Forum Psychoanalyse*, 7, pp. 98-110.

Deserno, H. (1990), *Die Analyse und das Arbeitsbündnis*, (Munich & Vienna).

Dewe, B. & H.-U. Otto (1987), 'Professionalisierung,' in: H. Eyferth, H. U. Otto & H. Thiersch (eds.), *Handbuch zur Sozialarbeit/Sozialpädagogik*, (Neuwied & Darmstadt), pp. 775-811.

Ermann, M. (1992), 'Die sogenannte Realbeziehung,' in: *Forum Psychoanalyse*, 8, pp. 281-94.

Faimberg, H. (1987), 'Die Ineinanderrückung (Telescoping) der Generationen. Zur Genealogie gewisser Identifizierungen,' in: *Jahrbuch der Psychoanalyse*, 20, pp. 114-42.

Freud, S. (1895), 'Studies on Hysteria,' SE Vol. II

— (1915a), 'Observations on Transference-Love,' SE Vol. XII, p.159

Jacoby, R. (1975), 'Negative Psychoanalyse und Marxismus,' in: *Psyche*, 29, pp. 961-90.

Körner, J. (1989), 'Kritik der therapeutischen Ich-Spaltung,' in: *Psyche*, 43, pp. 385-96.

— (1990), 'Die Bedeutung kasuistischer Darstellungen in der Psychoanalyse,' in: G.Jüttemann (ed.), *Komparative Kasuistik*, (Heidelberg), pp.93-103.

— (1990), 'Übertragung und Gegenübertragung, eine Einheit im Widerspruch,' in: *Forum Psychoanalyse*, 6, pp. 87-104.

Kutter, P., R. Páramo-Ortega & P. Zagermann (eds.) (1988), *Die psychoanalytische Haltung. Auf der Suche nach dem Selbstbild der Psychoanalyse*, (Munich & Vienna).

Mertens, W. (1992), *Kompendium Psychoanalytischer Grundbegriffe*, (Munich).

Meyer, A. E, (1994), 'Nieder mit der Novelle als Psychoanalysedarstellung – Hoch lebe die Interaktionsgeschichte,' in: *Zeitschrift für Psychosomatische Medizin und Psychoanalyse*, 40, pp. 77-98.

Niemeyer, Ch. (1990), 'Zum Verhältnis von Berufsethik und Adressatenethik in der Sozialpädagogik – unter besonderer Berücksichtigung des Beitrages von Hermann Nohl,' in: B. Müller & H. Thiersch (eds.), *Gerechtigkeit und Selbstverwirklichung. Moralprobleme im sozialpädagogischen Handeln*, (Freiburg), pp. 85-121.

Raguse, K. (1992), 'Psychoanalytische Situation und Abstinenz. Reflexionen zu Fiktion und Realität in der Analyse,' unpublished lecture.

Sandler, A.-M. (1988), 'Comments on therapeutic and countertherapeutic factors in psychoanalytic technique,' in: *Bulletin of the Anna Freud Centre*, 11, pp. 3 -13.

Sandler, J. (1976), 'Gegenübertragung und die Bereitschaft zur Rollenübernahme,' in: *Psyche*, 30, pp.297-305.

Schwendenwein, W. (1990), 'Profession - Professionalisierung - professionelles Handeln,' in: L. M. Alisch, J. Baumert & K. Beck (eds.), *Professionswissen und Professionalisierung. Braunschweiger Studien zur Sozialarbeitswissenschaft* 28, pp.359-81.

Spence, D. P. (1982), 'Narrative truth and theoretical truth,' in: *Psychoanalytic Quarterly*, 51, pp.43-69.

Terhart, E. (1990), 'Professionen in Organisationen: Institutionelle Bedingungen der Entwicklung von Professionswissen,' in: L. M. Alisch, J. Baumert & K. Beck (eds.), *Professionswissen und Professionalisierung. Braunschweiger Studien zur Sozialarbeitswissenschaft*, 28, pp.151-70.

Thomä, H. & H. Kächele (1985), *Lehrbuch der psychoanalytischen Therapie*, vol. 1, (Berlin, Heidelberg & New York).

Titze, H. (1989), 'Professionalisierung,' in: D. Lenzen (ed.), *Pädagogische Grundbegriffe*, vol. 2, (Reinbek), pp. 1270-2.

BIBLIOGRAPHIES

HELMUT REIFF

Bachelard, G. (1971), *Epistemology*, (Frankfurt, Berlin & Vienna, 1974).

Bandura, A, (1979), *Sozial-kognitive Lerntheorie*, (Stuttgart).

Black, M. (1979), 'More about Metaphor,' in: Ortony (ed.), *Metaphor and Thought*, (Cambridge).

Bourdieu, P. (1979), *Distinction*, (RKP, London, 1986).

Capelle, W. (1968), *Die Vorsokratiker*, (Stuttgart).

Bruder, K. (1993), *Subjektivitä und Postmoderne*, (Frankfurt/M.).

Cremerius, J. (1993), in: *DPV-Info*No. 13, pp.7-10.

Deleuze, G. & F. Guattari (1972), *Anti-Oedipus*, (Athlone, London, 1984).

Diels, H. (1963), *Die Fragmente der Vorsokratiker*, (Hamburg).

Freud, S. (1900a), *The Interpretation of Dreams*, SE Vols IV-V

— (1933a [1932]), *New Introductory Lectures on Psycho-Analysis,* SE Vol. XXII, p.3

— (1938 [1940e]), 'The Splitting of the Ego in the Process of Defence,' SE Vol. XXIII, p.273

Hartmann, H. (1964), *Ich-Psychologie*, (Stuttgart, 1972).

Holenstein, E. (1975), *Roman Jakobsons phänomenologischer Strukturalismus*, (Frankfurt/M.)

Illich, I. (1976), Limits to Medicine, (Boyars, London).

Jappe, G. (1992), in: *DPV-Info*, No. 12, pp.11-7.

Lacan, J. (1966), *Ecrits*, (Tavistock, 1980).

Novottny, H. (1992), *Eigenzeit*, (Frankfurt/M.)

Piaget, J. (1950), *Child's Conception of the World*, (Palladin, 1973).

Reich, W. (1932), *The Invasion of Compulsory Sex-Morality*, (Pelican Books, 1975).

Tübinger Akademie für Verhaltenstherapie (TAVT) (1994), *Fort- und Weiterbildung in Verhaltenstherapie*, (Tübingen).

Watson, J. B. (1930), *Behaviorism*, (Norton, 1980).

Winnicott, D. W. (1970), *Playing and Reality*, (Penguin, Harmondsworth, 1974).

MICHAEL WIRSCHING

Baudrillard, J. (1988), 'Die Simulation,' in: W. Welsch (ed.), *Wege aus der Moderne. Schlüsseltexte aus der Postmoderne-Diskussion*, (Weinheim), pp. 153-62.

— (1989), Cool Memories, Verso, 1990.

Beck, U. (1986), *Risk Society*, (London).

— with E. Beck-Gernsheim (1990), *Das ganz normale Chaos der Liebe*, (Frankfurt).

Breuer, J. and S. Freud (1895), *Studies on Hysteria*, SE vol. II

Cremerius, J. (1987), 'Für eine psychoanalysegerechte Ausbildung,' in: *Psyche*, 41, pp. 1067-94.

Dürrenmatt, F. (1991), 'Menschheit im Universum der Katastrophen', in: *Frankfurter Allgemeine Zeitung*, January 12, 1991.

Ellenberger, H. F. (1973), Die Entdeckung des Unbewussten, vol. 1, (Bern, Stuttgart & Vienna).

Foerster, H. von (1985), 'Entdecken oder Erfinden. Wie lässt sich Verstehen verstehen?', in: H. Gumin & A. Mohler (eds.), *Einführung in den Konstruktivismus*, (Munich), pp. 27-68.

Garfield, S.L. & A. E. Bergin (1996), 'Introduction and historical Overview', in: their (eds.), *Handbook of Psychotherapy and Behavior Change*, (New York, Wiley), pp. 3-22.

Glucksmann, A. (1991), 'Warum ist die Depression gut für Europa, Monsieur Glucksmann?' An interview by Renée Zucker, in: *Frankfurter Allgemeine Zeitung*, January 11, 1991.

Grawe, K. (1988), 'Psychotherapeutische Verfahren im wissenschaftlichen Vergleich,' in: *Praxis der Psychotherapie und Psychosomatik*, 33, pp. 153-67

Habermas, J. (1973), *Knowledge and Human Interests*, (Heinemann Educational, 1978).

— (1985), *Die neue Unübersichtlichkeit*, (Frankfurt/M.).

Hassan, I. (1988), 'Postmoderne heute,' in: W. Welsch (ed.), *Wege aus der Moderne. Schlüsseltexte aus der Postmoderne-Diskussion*, (Weinheim), pp. 47-56.

House, J., K. R. Landis & D. Umberson (1988), 'Social relationship and health,' in: *Science*, 241, pp. 540-5.

Kuhn, T. S. (1970), The Structure of Scientific Revolutions, (Univ. of Chicago, Chicago).

Luborsky, L., B. Singer & L. Luborsky (1975), 'Comparative studies of psychotherapies,' in: *Arch. Gen. Psychiatry*, 32, pp. 995-1008.

Luhmann, N. (1984), *Soziale Systeme. Grundriss einer allgemeinen Theorie*, (Frankfurt/M.).

Marcuse, H. (1970), *Kultur und Gesellschaft*, vol. 1, (Frankfurt/M.)

Maturana, H.R. (1985), *Erkennen: Die Organisation und Verkörperung von Wirklichkeit*, (Braunschweig).

Mitscherlich, A. & M. Mitscherlich (1968), *Die Unfähigkeit zu trauern*, (Piper, Munich).

Orlinsky, D. E. & K. 1. Howard (1986), 'Process and outcome in psychotherapy,' in: S. L. Garfield & A. E. Bergin (eds.), *Handbook of Psychotherapy and Behavior Change*, (New York), pp. 311-81.

Ortega, R. P. (1991), 'Die Verarmung der Psychoanalyse. Über den Verfall der psychoanalytischen Ausbildung,' in: *Psyche*, 45, p. 61-83.

Parin, P. (1981), 'Das Ende der endlichen Analyse,' in: U. Ehebald (ed.), *Humanität und Technik in der Psychoanalyse*, (Bern).

Schepank, H. (1987), *Psychogene Erkrankungen der Stadtbevölkerung*. Eine tiefenpsychologisch-epidemiologische Feldstudie in Mannheim, (Berlin, Heidelberg & New York).

Schmale, A. H, & G. L. Engel (1974), 'A role of conservation-withdrawal in depressive reactions,' in: E. J. Anthony & T. Benedek (eds.), *Depression and Human Existence*, (Boston), pp. 183-98.

Schott, H. (1986), 'Psychoanalyse und Psychotherapie. Ihre historische Auseinandersetzung und die Folgen,' in: *Psychother. Med. Psychol.*, 36, pp. 253-58.

Seidler, E. (1990), 'Was ist ein Psychotherapeut? Historische Anmerkungen zu einem aktuellen Thema,' in G. Sonneck (ed.): *Das Berufsbild des Psychotherapeuten. Kosten und Nutzen der Psychotherapie*, pp.10-16.

Smith, M. L., G. V. Glass & T. I. Miller (1980), The Benefit of Psychotherapy, (Baltimore)

Uexküll, T. von & W. Wesiak (1988), *Theorie der Humanmedizin*, (Munich, Vienna & Baltimore).

Index